CONTENTS

CONTENTS

Animal ENCYCLOPEDIA

Birds · Insects

Mammals · Fish

Reptiles · Amphibians

A visual guide to the creatures of the world

ABOUT ANIMALS

Animals are a large group of multi-cellular organisms. They are different from human beings. Animals can be divided into five groups: mammals, reptiles, amphibians, birds and fish.

Mammalia

There are more than 4,000 kinds of mammals in the world. They are warm-blooded animals and are found in all parts of the world. They are the most intelligent creatures on earth and can **adapt** their body temperature to different climatic conditions and temperatures.

Some amphibians begin their life in the water. Frogs for example begin their life as tadpoles in the water.

Amphibians and Reptiles

Both amphibians and reptiles are cold-blooded animals that breathe through lungs. Amphibians, however, can also live underwater. Frogs and toads are amphibians while snakes and lizards are called reptiles.

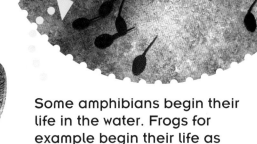
Kangaroos belong to a class of mammals known as marsupials.

In Air and in Water

Birds are warm-blooded animals that lay eggs. Unlike other animals, birds can fly using wings. However, there are some birds, like the ostrich, that do not fly. Fish, on the other hand, stay only in water. They will die if they are taken out of water. They breathe through **gills**.

CANINES

Canine (or Canidae) is the name for the dog family that includes wolves, foxes, coyotes and jackals. There are about 400 species of dog in the world.

The Fox

The fox is the most common mammal found in the world. It is much smaller than other canines. The fox is also a solitary animal, unlike many other canines that live in groups. The red fox is the most common species.

The sandy coloured coat of the Fennec fox allows it to blend into the desert surroundings.

A fox's large ears help to dissipate heat and detect movement.

Fun Facts

The Arctic fox is the only member of the Canidae family that changes the colour of its coat according to the season. While its winter coat is white, it has a bluish grey coat in summer.

The Fennec fox is the smallest fox in the world.

- The dingo is an Australian wild dog, found in all states of Australia except Tasmania.
- Wolves have two layers of fur. The first layer helps to repel water and dust while the second layer helps to keep the body warm.
- Fox hunting began as a sport in the 16th century in the UK.

Wolves

Wolves belong to the same family as domesticated dogs. They are found in remote forests and hunt in packs. They feed on large and medium-sized animals like sheep, pigs and deer. There are two main species of wolves - the red and the grey.

Grey wolves are the largest Canines.

DID YOU KNOW?

Foxes store their food under leaves, snow or soil to eat later.

BIG CATS

The big cats are the largest members of the cat family and include tigers, lions, leopards and jaguars. They are distinguished by their ability to roar.

The Striped Prowler

The tiger is the largest member of the big cat family. They grow up to 4 m (13 ft) in length and weigh over 300 kg (660 lbs). They are **nocturnal** animals and hunt for their prey at night. They have strong eyesight and a keen sense of smell. There are five different species of tiger in the world.

The Royal Bengal tiger is found in the rainforests and grasslands of Bangladesh, Bhutan, Burma, China, India and Nepal.

The Royal Bengal tiger has orange and white fur with black stripes.

Second in Charge

The lion is the second largest living cat. Unlike other big cats, lions live in big groups of about 15 animals, known as a pride. Male lions are recognised by the thick mane of brown hair that encircles their head and neck.

Lions are the most social of the big cats, living in groups.

- Though the leopard is the smallest member of the big cat family, it is still the best and strongest climber of all the large cats.
- The Siberian tiger (also known as the Amur) is a rare species of the tiger family. Only 7,000 Siberians are left in the world today.
- Cougars, also known as panthers or pumas, are the largest cats that can purr!

Fun Facts

Tigers have more than a hundred stripes on their body but no two tigers have the same number and pattern of stripes.

DID YOU KNOW?

Lions are the laziest of all the big cats. They sleep and rest for more than 20 hours a day!

HOOVED ANIMALS

Hooved animals are also known as ungulates. They can be odd-toed or even-toed, depending on the number of toes.

The camel's large nostrils store water vapour and help prevent water loss.

Fun Facts

All camels have a very unique stomach. Unlike humans or other animals, their stomachs are divided into three compartments, helping them in the digestion of their food.

Ship of the Desert

Most camels live in the desert, but some species are found in other arid areas like mountains. They can survive for a long time without water. Their **hump** is made of fatty tissues, which helps them control their body temperature and also act as an energy reserve to help them withstand long periods of heat and dehydration.

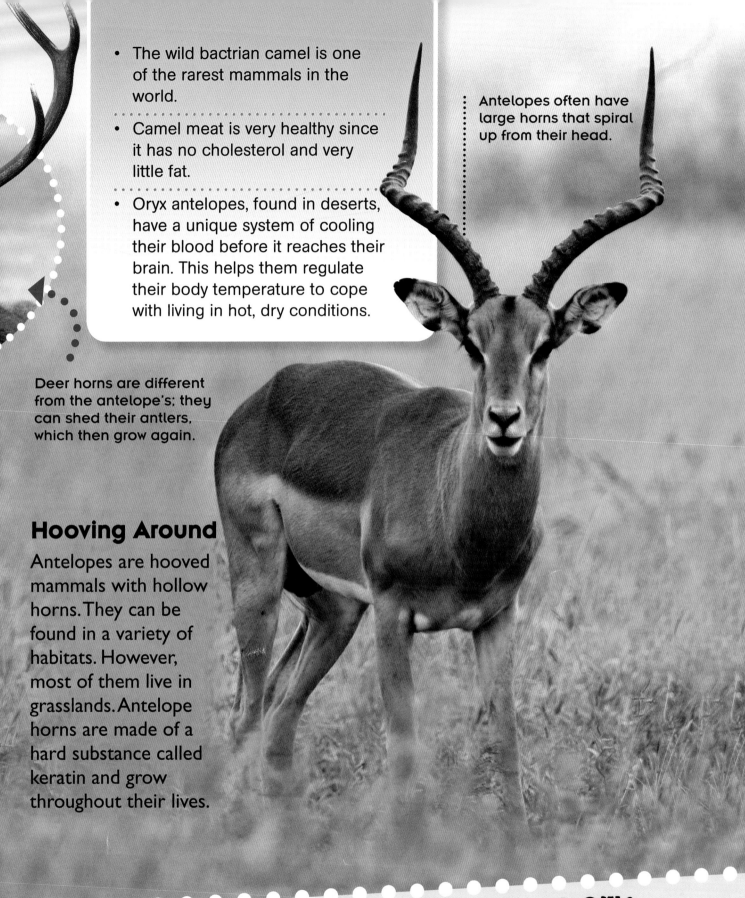

- The wild bactrian camel is one of the rarest mammals in the world.
- Camel meat is very healthy since it has no cholesterol and very little fat.
- Oryx antelopes, found in deserts, have a unique system of cooling their blood before it reaches their brain. This helps them regulate their body temperature to cope with living in hot, dry conditions.

Antelopes often have large horns that spiral up from their head.

Deer horns are different from the antelope's; they can shed their antlers, which then grow again.

Hooving Around

Antelopes are hooved mammals with hollow horns. They can be found in a variety of habitats. However, most of them live in grasslands. Antelope horns are made of a hard substance called keratin and grow throughout their lives.

DID YOU KNOW?

Camels were used by the Bedouins in war against the Persians in the 7th century B.C.

MONKEYS AND APES

Monkeys and apes are mammals. They belong to the same category that human beings are a part of – **primates.**

Orangutans are apes that live in the rainforests of Borneo and Sumatra.

Their Habitat

Monkeys are found in many types of habitat – from forests and deserts to grasslands and mountains. They are found in all parts of the world. Apes, however, live only in the rainforests of Africa and Asia.

A group of monkeys is called a troop.

Fun Facts

Chimpanzees have a cheeky trick of poking a long stick into an ant hill. When the ants have crawled onto the stick, the chimpanzee takes the stick out and licks up all the ants!

Some monkeys have long tails that help them hold on to branches as they swing between trees.

Their Differences

Monkeys are different from apes in many ways. Most monkeys have tails but apes do not have tails. Apes can use their hands to swing from branch to branch. Monkeys cannot do that. Instead, they run on the tree branches.

- A monkey's eyes are rounder and closer together than human eyes.
- In some monkeys, the arms are as long as the legs.
- Monkeys do not catch a cold!
- Experts say that vervet monkeys have their own language.

A male gorilla is more than ten times stronger than an average adult man.

Male gorillas typically have a patch of silver hair on their back.

Gorillas walk on all four limbs, putting pressure on their knuckles. This is called knuckle-walking.

DID YOU KNOW?

Monkeys eat bananas just like us. They first peel off the skin and then eat the fruit.

ELEPHANTS

Elephants are the largest living land animals. They live in secluded areas, far from human beings.

Trunking Around

Elephants weigh between 90-120 kg (200-265 lbs) when they are born. Elephants live in small groups. They eat roots, bark, grass, leaves and fruit. They have been known to uproot entire trees to reach the fruit!

Close Cousins

The Asian elephant is smaller than its African counterpart and has smaller ears. Despite their weight, elephants walk very quietly, distributing their weight by a thick cushion of tissue on the base of their foot.

When travelling, elephants move in a single file.

- Female elephants are fertile to have **offspring** up to the age of around 55.
- Elephants have a very acute sense of hearing.
- The size of an elephant's family depends on the amount of food available in the area and how well they get along with each other.

RHINOS AND HIPPOS

Rhinoceroses and hippopotamuses are also classified as ungulates or hooved animals. The hippo lives on riverbanks. The rhino has horns.

Horned Nose

Rhinos are huge, with most species weighing nearly one tonne! They have a large horn above the nose and a tough exterior skin between 1.5-5 cm (0.5-2 in) thick. There are five types of rhinos: white, black, Indian, Sumatran and Javan.

The rhino's horn is made of keratin and was traditionally used in Asian medicines.

Fun Facts

Even when a hippo is sleeping underwater, it raises its head to breathe without even waking up!

River Horse

The hippo (literally meaning 'river horse') spends its days in water and comes to the land at night to eat. A hippo can spend long periods underwater, but typically surfaces every 3 to 5 minutes to breathe. They are native to Africa.

- Hippos often scare away their **predator**s by opening their mouth and showing their canines, which can grow up to 50 cm (20 in) in length.
- The Javan rhino is one of the rarest and most **endangered** animal in the world.
- Hippos secrete a red substance from their skin, which acts like a natural sunscreen.

BEARS

Bears are solitary animals, usually active in the early morning or at dusk. Bears are usually found in parts of the Americas, Europe and Asia.

The grizzly bear, like other brown bears, can be distinguished by the hump on its back, made up of muscle. This bundle of muscles gives the bear the force to dig its forelimbs into its prey.

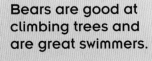

Bears are good at climbing trees and are great swimmers.

The Big Brown Bear

The brown bear can be found all over Europe, Asia and North America. Despite its name, some species can be brown, black and even blonde. Brown bears are very powerful animals and can break the necks of even large prey when they hunt.

Fun Facts

Hibernating female bears don't even wake up when they give birth to their cubs during winter. The baby bear cubs crawl into a position where they can feed themselves from their mother soon after birth.

White as Snow

Polar bears live around the Arctic Ocean. They have a thick layer of fat under their skin, which helps them keep warm in cold climates and also helps them float while swimming. They also have two layers of fur.

Despite their size, bears are fast runners.

- While the brown bear, the black bear and the panda rely on fruit, nuts and berries as their primary source of food, it is only the Polar bear that is mainly carnivorous in nature, feeding on seals.
- Pandas do not hibernate like other species of bears
- The grizzly bear is the largest meat eater in the world.

The Polar bear lives mainly on seal meat.

The grizzly bear gets its name from the grey or silver tips of the hair on its back.

DID YOU KNOW?

Brown bears eat almost continuously during the summer and autumn as they get ready for winter.

RODENTS

Rodents are the largest order of mammals in terms of number of species. They have sharp incisor teeth that grow continuously and must be kept short by gnawing. They are found everywhere except in Antarctica.

Notorious Nibblers

Mice are the most common rodents and are found across the world. They typically prefer seeds and grains. They can also survive for long periods of time with little or no water, obtaining their water from the food that they eat. They are mainly nocturnal animals.

- Hamsters are named after the German word, *hamstern*, which means to hoard. This is due to the fact that these creatures carry food in their cheek pouches and hide it away safely.

- Pet gerbils have to be provided with things they can chew to prevent their very sharp incisors from growing too long.

Mice are usually most active at night.

20

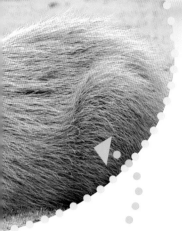

The capybara is the world's largest rodent. It can grow as big as a dog.

Gentle Guinea Pigs

Small rodents like hamsters, gerbils and guinea pigs have become popular as family pets. Guinea pigs are the largest of all pet rodents. They are considered to be very good pets and seldom bite or scratch even if stressed or disturbed. They vary widely in hair composition and colour. Some have a smooth coat while others have a ruffled coat.

If guinea pigs don't get food to chew on, they chew on their own hair or even on plastic or cloth.

Their mild nature makes guinea pigs very popular as pets.

DID YOU KNOW ?

Millions of people died in Europe in the 14th century because of a terrible disease carried by rats and transmitted by fleas. This was known as the Black Death.

BIRDS

Birds are warm-blooded vertebrates that lay eggs. There are more than 10,000 living species of birds in the world. All birds have feathers, beaks and wings, but not all can fly.

Diet

While most birds are plant eating creatures, there are some birds that are meat eating. These are known as raptors or birds of prey. Vultures, hawks, eagles and kites are all birds of prey.

Most birds are active in the day. However, some birds like the owl are active at night.

Songbirds

Birds that have musical voices are called songbirds. They have specially developed vocal cords or syringes, which they use to produce sounds or 'songs'. They also have a special section in their brain which helps them learn their songs.

Fly Away

Flying allows birds to travel, hunt for food and avoid predators. Birds have a very light skeleton, strong flying muscles and wings. The shape and size of the wing determines the distance and type of flight for birds. Feathers provide insulation and help maintain body temperature.

FLIGHTLESS BIRDS

While most birds can fly, there are some birds that do not fly. Even though they look like birds, their legs are adapted in many instances to help them cover long distances by walking or running.

A kiwi may be the size of a chicken, but its egg is up to six times larger than a chicken's!

Running Bird

The ostrich is the largest flightless bird in the world. Found in parts of Africa, they weigh 113-181 kg (250-400 lbs) and stand 1.8-2.4 m (6-8 ft) tall. They have two-toed feet that allow them to run fast and escape from predators.

New Zealander

The kiwi is also a flightless bird. This protected and endangered national bird of New Zealand is nocturnal by nature. The kiwi's beak is almost one-third the length of its body. It uses its excellent sense of smell to hunt for worms, insects, berries and seeds.

The long neck of the ostrich gives it the ability to see a greater distance across the plains.

- To produce her huge egg, the female kiwi must eat three times her normal food intake for a month!

- Emus, like the ostrich, drink large quantities of water and can drink up to 70 mouthfuls of water at one go.

- Contrary to popular belief, ostriches do not bury their head in the sand when they see danger.

DID YOU KNOW ?

Emu eggs are dark green in colour. Each egg can weigh up to 0.68 kgs (1.5 lbs).

REPTILES

Reptiles are cold-blooded animals and are covered with scales or plates, as apposed to skin or feathers. The majority of reptiles are **oviparous**, meaning they lay eggs, from which their young are born.

- Four main orders of reptiles are recognised: **Crocodilia** (including crocodiles and alligators); **Sphenodontia** (including tuatara); **Squamata** (including lizards and snakes); **Testudines** (including turtles and tortoises).

- Most reptiles lay eggs, but some lizards and snakes give birth to live young.

- The horned lizard is known to defend itself from its enemies by spraying them with blood from the corner of its eye.

Slithering Around

Lizards make up the largest group of reptiles. There are over 3,700 species of lizards spread all over the world. Lizards also have dry, scaly skin and clawed feet. They usually feed on insects, with some being vegetarians.

Komodo dragons can eat up to 80 per cent of their body weight during a single meal.

The Komodo dragon is the largest lizard in the world.

The mouth of the Komodo dragon is full of poisonous bacteria capable of killing a man.

Mobile Homes

Turtles are also classified as reptiles. They have a hard shell on their back that acts like armour. Most turtles live in the sea. Turtles also have a beak but do not have any teeth. Their hard jaw rim helps them cut and chew food. Tortoises also belong to the same family as turtles but live on land.

Tortoises can draw their head, legs and tails into their hard shell when they sense danger.

Fun Facts

The average life span of a common snapping turtle is about 40 years. However, the giant tortoise is known to live for as long as 170 years!

DID YOU KNOW ?

Chameleons have an amazing ability to change the colour of their body instantly.

SNAKES

Snakes are also reptiles, but they do not have legs. They are cold-blooded and usually nocturnal in nature. Some species, however, can be found in the day.

Slithering Around

Snakes do not have external ears but can sense sound through **vibrations**. They have an inner ear and can feel the vibrations on the ground. The vibration is then passed onto the inner ear and helps them hunt. They also have smell sensors on the tips of their tongues and heat sensors, which help them in locating food.

Some snakes have a flap of skin on the side of their head. These flare out to form a hood and help scare predators away.

Fun Facts

Snakes do not hear a snake charmer. When we see a snake swaying to the music of the snake charmer it is actually moving to the vibrations of the charmer's movement.

Snakes have a transparent scale that covers the eye. The scale is frequently replaced by a new one helping the snake see clearly again.

Snakes have a flexible lower jaw that helps them swallow their prey whole.

Snakes use their nostrils only for breathing. They smell with their tongues.

26

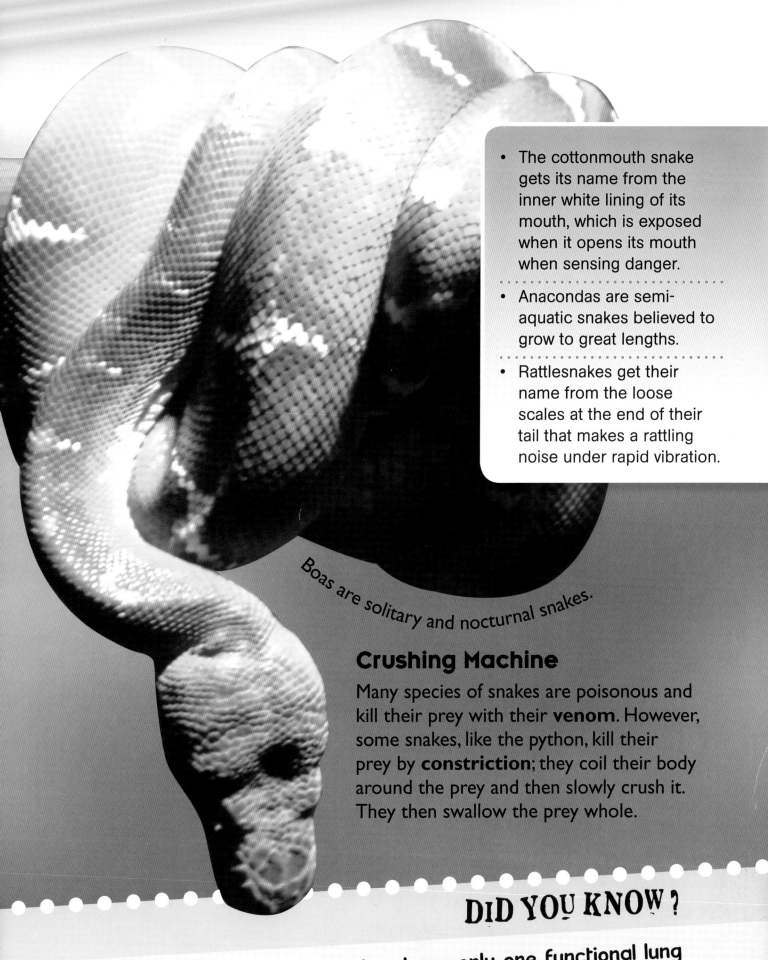

- The cottonmouth snake gets its name from the inner white lining of its mouth, which is exposed when it opens its mouth when sensing danger.

- Anacondas are semi-aquatic snakes believed to grow to great lengths.

- Rattlesnakes get their name from the loose scales at the end of their tail that makes a rattling noise under rapid vibration.

Boas are solitary and nocturnal snakes.

Crushing Machine

Many species of snakes are poisonous and kill their prey with their **venom**. However, some snakes, like the python, kill their prey by **constriction**; they coil their body around the prey and then slowly crush it. They then swallow the prey whole.

DID YOU KNOW?

Snakes have only one functional lung located on the right side of their body.

AMPHIBIANS

Amphibians can live on both land and in water. Most amphibians begin their life in water. Even fully grown, they cannot live all their life on land.

In Land and Water

Frogs, toads, and salamanders are all types of amphibians. Most amphibians are born in water, where the eggs are laid. Amphibians that are spawned in water do not have limbs and look more like fish. They breathe through gills and have tails to help them swim. Over time, their lungs and legs grow in a process known as **metamorphosis**.

A newt is a salamander that lives in the water as an adult.

Fun Facts

Most frogs live in and around water. However, there are also some types of frogs that never go near water and live only on land and even on trees, extracting moisture from the air!

There are more than 6,000 species of amphibians in the world.

28

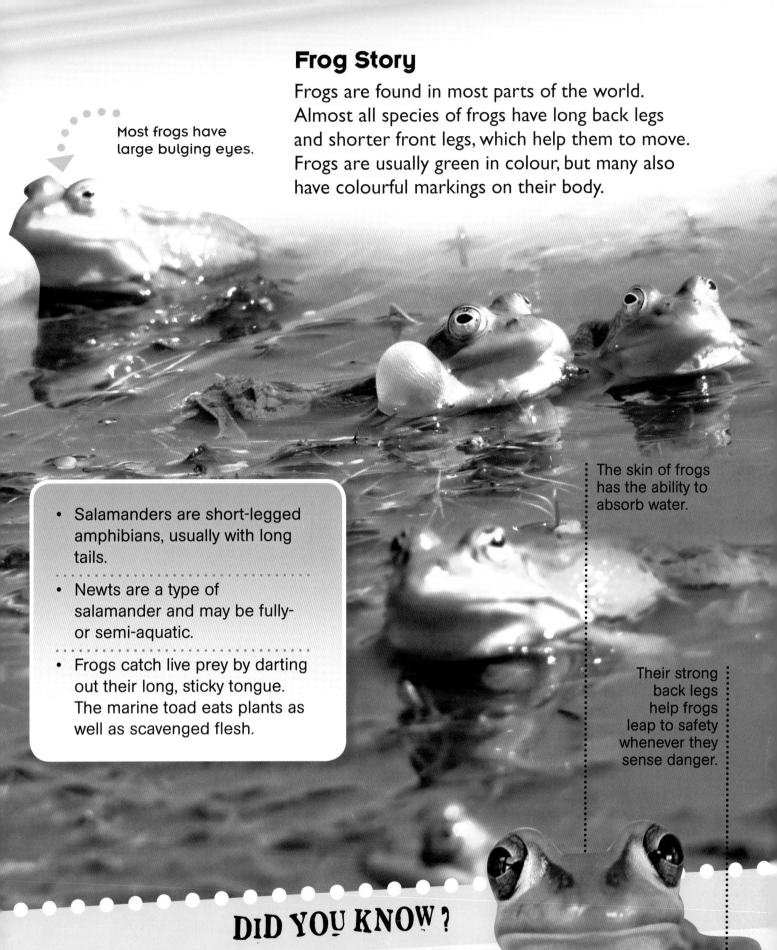

Frog Story

Frogs are found in most parts of the world. Almost all species of frogs have long back legs and shorter front legs, which help them to move. Frogs are usually green in colour, but many also have colourful markings on their body.

Most frogs have large bulging eyes.

The skin of frogs has the ability to absorb water.

- Salamanders are short-legged amphibians, usually with long tails.

- Newts are a type of salamander and may be fully- or semi-aquatic.

- Frogs catch live prey by darting out their long, sticky tongue. The marine toad eats plants as well as scavenged flesh.

Their strong back legs help frogs leap to safety whenever they sense danger.

DID YOU KNOW?

Some rainforest frogs are very poisonous. This poison has traditionally been used to tip arrows and darts.

SHARKS AND RAYS

The great white shark is the most feared of all sharks.

Sharks and rays are among some of the most feared and misunderstood creatures in the seas and oceans.

Sharks use their tail to provide thrust and speed while swimming.

The whale shark is the largest shark. It is also the largest fish in the world and can grow up to 15 m (50 ft) long!

Predators at Sea

Sharks are a type of fish. They do not have bones like other fish but are made up of cartilage – strong tissue as hard as bone. Sharks have a keen sense of smell and some can detect just a drop of blood from quite a distance. Many sharks also have keen eyesight.

Poisonous Sting

Stingrays are related to sharks and get their name from the **serrated**, poisonous spine that grows from their tail. Stingrays can grow as long as 4.6 m (15 ft). However, they normally only sting only in **self defence**.

Stingrays spend most of their time inactive, buried in the sand on the ocean floor.

- Stingrays are a family of fish and include several different species.
- There are about 368 species of sharks in the world.
- Some shark species are **oviparous** (egg-layers) and some are **viviparous**, giving birth to live pups.

CRABS AND SHELLFISH

Crustacea and molluscs are another type of marine life. They include crabs, lobsters, shrimps, and crayfish. The octopus is a type of mollusc.

Crustacea

The crab and the lobster are some of the most popular crustacea in the world. They have a soft inner body and a hard outer shell called an **exoskeleton**. The shell does not grow in size; rather, the outer shell is shed at regular intervals as a larger shell develops beneath.

Prey Suckers

The octopus is an invertebrate with a bag-shaped body, a large head and eight tentacles used to catch prey. Octopuses have the remarkable ability to change both the colour and the texture of their body. This helps them to merge into their surroundings and escape from enemies. Snails and slugs also belong to the same family as the octopus.

The octopus squirts out a black inky substance when it is threatened. It uses the resulting cloud to make its escape.

The horseshoe crab has changed very little in over 25 million years.

A crab's claws are known as chelae.

MARINE MAMMALS

There are about 120 species of mammals in the world that can be classified as marine mammals, including whales, dolphins and walruses.

A whale's tail fin is horizontal and not vertical like a shark's.

Whales

Whales are among the biggest living creatures in the world. Whales are warm-blooded and give birth to live young. They breathe air through lungs and have to surface at regular intervals to breathe in through blowholes situated on top of their heads. Baleen whales have a sieve-like structure, which they use to separate plankton from the water. The toothed whales have teeth and eat fish and squid.

- Dolphins and whales use sound waves to locate their food and other objects in the water.
- The killer whale (orca) is actually the largest dolphin and can grow up to 6.1 m (20 ft) long.
- The average bottlenose dolphin brain weighs 1.5 kgs (3.4 lbs) more than the human brain.

Dolphins

Dolphins belong to the same family (**cetaceans**) as whales but are physically different from them. They can be found in all oceans and seas and feed on small fish, squid, crabs, shrimps and lobsters. Dolphins are also social animals and live in large groups of 12 or more animals. These groups are known as pods.

Seals and Walruses

Walruses and seals are flippered mammals and belong to the family of pinnipeds. Walruses live in the Arctic Ocean and sub-Arctic seas of the Northern Hemisphere. Seals live in the Antarctic region.

Although they live in saltwater, dolphins do not drink water. They get their water from their food.

Dolphins are playful creatures, often racing through the water and jumping out of it.

Fun Facts

Dolphins have to be conscious to breath, meaning they can never fall asleep completely. Instead, they let one half of their brain sleep at a time.

DID YOU KNOW?

Dolphins can produce unique whistles that help individual dolphins recognise each other.

SPIDERS AND SCORPIONS

Spiders and scorpions belong to the family of arachnids. There are over 100,000 species of arachnids in the world. They are different from insects in many ways, including having eight legs instead of six.

Web Masters

Spiders are found in all parts of the world and in every kind of habitat. They can be found in many colours. They are carnivores and hunt their prey through their sticky webs or by other clever traps.

Most spiders are extremely sensitive to sound and vibrations.

Spiders do not have claws but some have poisonous fangs.

The body of a spider is divided into two main parts, the thorax and abdomen.

Fun Facts

Some spiders have stripes and blotches on their body. This is a technique called *disruptive colouration* and helps them merge into the background and escape from predators.

Not all spiders are a dull black or brown.

- Scorpions usually eat insects. When food is scarce they have the amazing ability to slow down their metabolism and eat one third their normal amount of food.

- Though scorpions can live without food and even in harsh conditions, they cannot survive in areas where there is no loose soil.

- The jumping spider gets more than 90 per cent of its food from solid plant material produced by acacias.

Pincer Attack

Scorpions are closely related to spiders, mites and ticks. Scorpions are found in deserts, in the Brazilian rainforests and even the Himalayan mountains! Most scorpions are nocturnal by nature and (contrary to popular belief) are not aggressive towards humans, unless provoked!

Scorpions navigate using sensory hairs and slit organs on their legs.

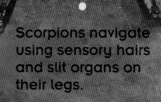

DID YOU KNOW?

There are almost 2,000 species of scorpions but only 30-40 species are poisonous enough to kill a human.

CREEPY CRAWLIES

Insects make up the largest group of creatures on earth. Eight out of every ten of all species are insects!

Hard Life

Insects are **arthropods**, meaning they have joint legs and a tough cover known as an exoskeleton outside their body. Confusingly, all insects are arthropods but not all arthropods are insects! The hard exoskeleton supports the body of the insect and helps protect the soft inner parts.

Parts and More

Most insects are born as eggs and grow into a larva, called a nymph. The larva becomes a pupa before becoming an adult. An insect's body consists of the head, thorax and abdomen. The head has a pair of antennae, eyes and a mouth. The thorax supports the legs and wings while the abdomen helps digest food.

- Insects that live in large colonies are known as social insects. Ants and bees are social insects.

- Different insects lay their eggs in different places. While some lay their eggs inside plant stems, some insects, like the beetle, lay their eggs on dead animals.

- Some insects, including mosquitos, lice and bedbugs are known as pests. However, there are some that are helpful to us, such as bees.

A queen bee can lay over 1,000 eggs in a day.

While some insects have simple eyes, most have compound eyes consisting of six-sided lenses.

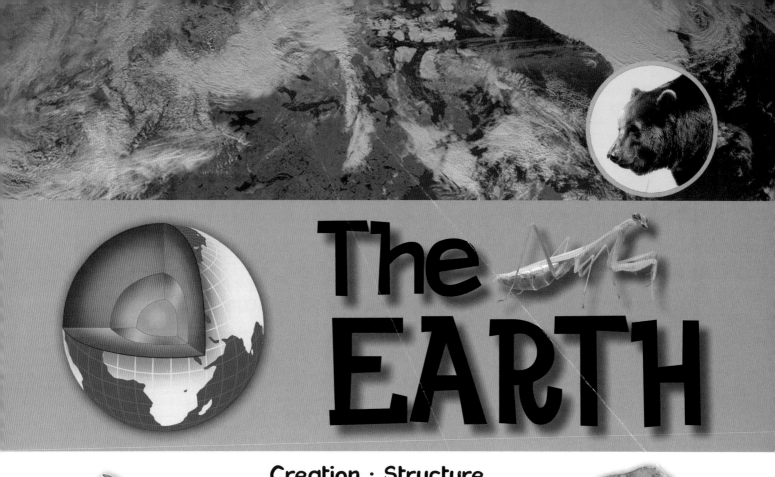

The EARTH

Creation · Structure

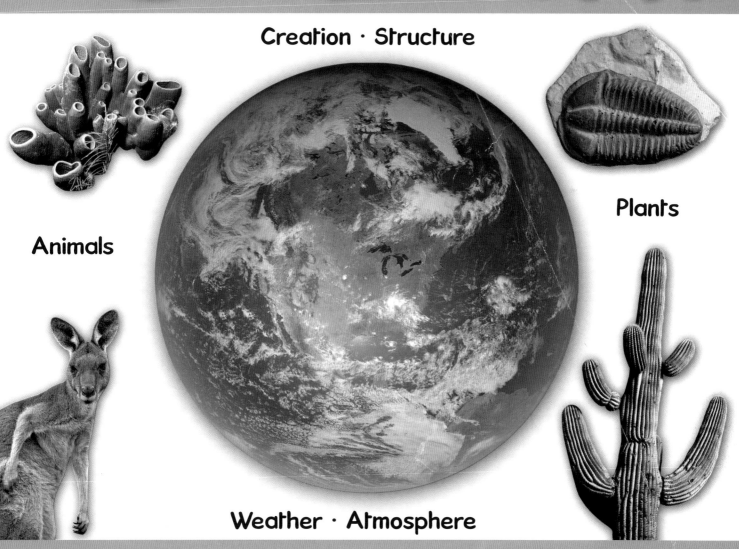

Animals

Plants

Weather · Atmosphere

A visual guide to our amazing planet

THE EARTH'S BEGINNING

We live on the Earth. It is a planet that is a part of a group of planets that go around the Sun.

That's the line-up

The Earth and seven other planets in our solar system go around the Sun that lights up your day. Right next to the Sun is Mercury. Then come Venus, Earth, Mars, Jupiter, Saturn, Uranus and, finally, Neptune.

The Earth is special. It is the only planet we know of that has life on it. Many smaller bodies also go around the Sun. These are called dwarf planets, comets, meteoroids and **asteroids**.

Each planet has a fixed path around the Sun.

Fun Facts

From 1930 Pluto was believed to be the ninth planet of our solar system. In 2006 Pluto was removed from the list for being too small. It is now called a dwarf planet or a Kuiper Belt object.

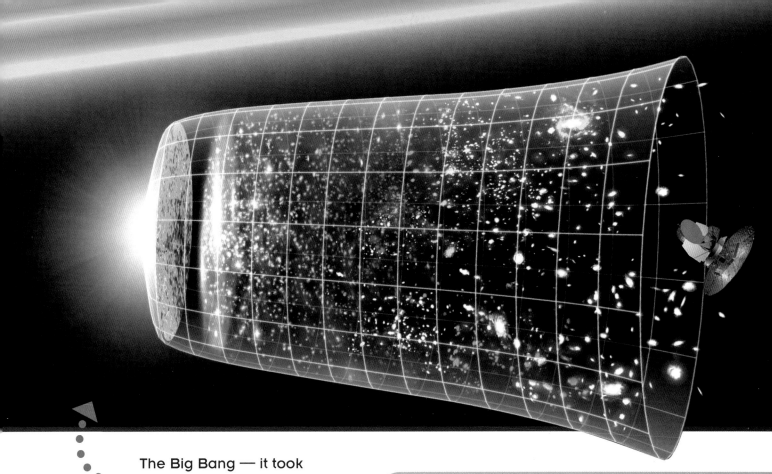

The Big Bang — it took less than a second and the universe was formed.

How it began

All the planets and stars were once inside a tiny, hot bubble. About 14 billion years ago (that is 14,000,000,000 years!) the bubble burst and particles rushed out of it to form stars. The explosion was so strong that they are still moving away from the bubble. This is called the Big Bang theory. At the time of the Big Bang, the Universe was 1,000 billion degrees Kelvin hot. In one hundredth of a second, it cooled to 100 billion degrees Kelvin.

- Earth and Mercury are the two **densest** planets in the Solar System. These planets have particles that are more packed together than other planets.
- Though the planet is called Earth, only about thirty per cent of its surface is actually 'earth'. The rest is all water.
- From a distance, the Earth looks the brightest of all planets, because its waters reflect the sunlight.

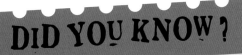
DID YOU KNOW ?

In one second, the Earth travels about 30 km (19 miles) around the Sun.

THE EARTH'S STRUCTURE

Have you ever dug a hole in the ground? You'd find soil, pebbles and rocks. But what you see is just the uppermost layer of the Earth.

Three-tiered Cake

The Earth has three layers. Not all of the Earth is cool enough to live on. Deep down is the core or the centre of the Earth. The inner core, which is the hottest part of the Earth, is made up of solid metals like iron and nickel. It is about 1,588 miles (2,556 km) in diameter.

The outer core is also made of iron, but it is liquid. It is about 2,746 miles (4,420 km) thick. Just above the core is the mantle or the middle layer. The inner layer of the mantle is liquid, and so it moves. The outer mantle is cooler and firm.

The mantle that lies below the crust constitutes almost two-thirds of the Earth's mass

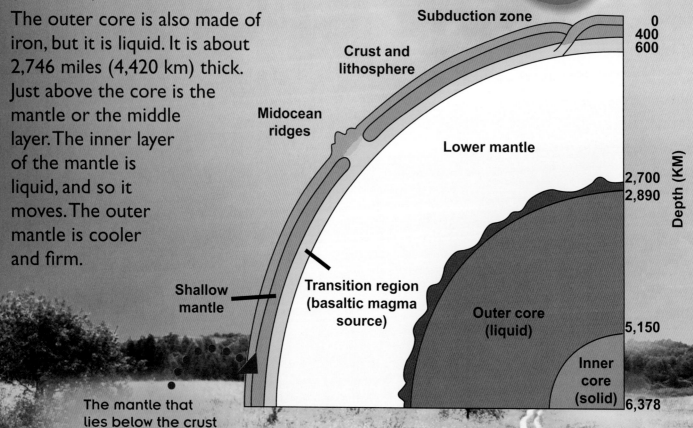

Subduction zone

Crust and lithosphere

Midocean ridges

Lower mantle

Shallow mantle

Transition region (basaltic magma source)

Outer core (liquid)

Inner core (solid)

Depth (KM)

0
400
600

2,700
2,890

5,150

6,378

That's where we live!

The Earth's surface is called the crust. It is the thinnest layer of the Earth. The crust is made up of rocks like granite and water. On the surface are oceans. These cover 70 per cent of the Earth's outermost cover. Some of these oceans can be as deep as 4 km (2.5 miles) in places. As massive as it may seem, the crust makes up less than one per cent of the Earth's total volume.

- Although the crust is a thin layer, it stretches for kilometres.
- As the Earth's plates move, the land mass of the continents changes. The first ever continent was called Pangea.
- About 245 million years ago in the Triassic Period, the Pangea split when the plates moved away to form the continents of Asia, Africa, Antarctica, Australia, Europe, and North and South America.
- That why the continents look like pieces a giant jigsaw puzzle.

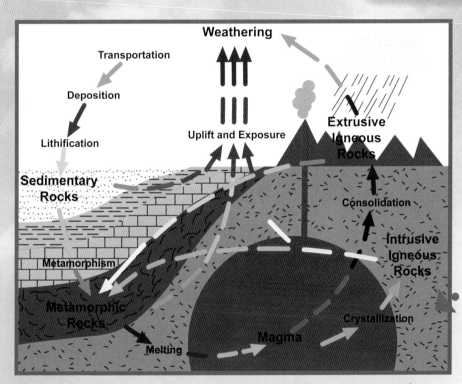

Weathering

Transportation

Deposition

Lithification

Uplift and Exposure

Extrusive Igneous Rocks

Sedimentary Rocks

Consolidation

Intrusive Igneous Rocks

Metamorphism

Crystallization

Metamorphic Rocks

Melting

Magma

The Earth's plates

Does the Earth look like one large sheet of soil? It is really made of large sections called continental plates. These plates move slowly over the mantle, covering a few inches in a year.

The Earth's crust is thickest below the continents.

THE SUN AND LIFE ON EARTH

For billions of years, Earth has had everything needed to support life. Life needs oxygen to breathe, water and the right temperature. It also needs a certain amount of gravity to keep us on the ground.

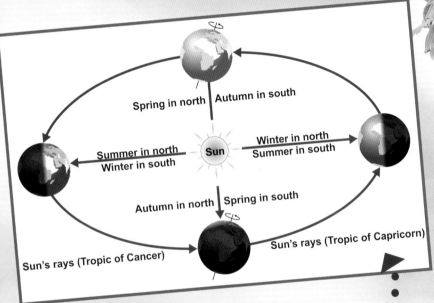

Spring in north | Autumn in south

Summer in north
Winter in south

Sun

Winter in north
Summer in south

Autumn in north | Spring in south

Sun's rays (Tropic of Cancer)

Sun's rays (Tropic of Capricorn)

The Earth going around the Sun.

Neither too near, nor too far

The Earth is just the right distance from the Sun for us to live on it. If we were any closer, like Mercury or Venus, it would be too hot for life. Were we further away, it would be too cold for life.

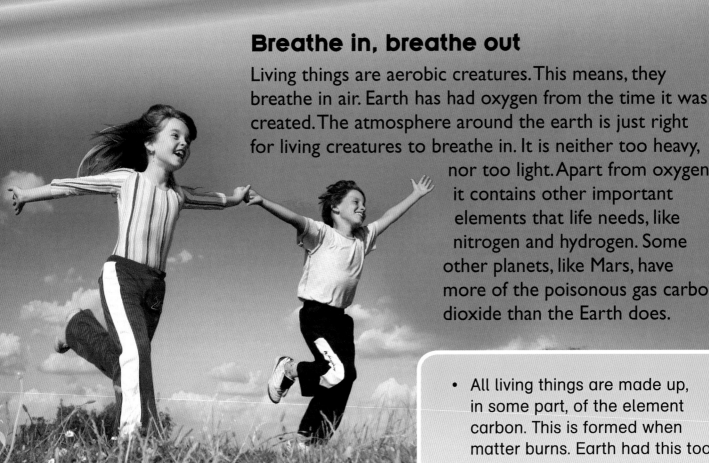

Breathe in, breathe out

Living things are aerobic creatures. This means, they breathe in air. Earth has had oxygen from the time it was created. The atmosphere around the earth is just right for living creatures to breathe in. It is neither too heavy, nor too light. Apart from oxygen, it contains other important elements that life needs, like nitrogen and hydrogen. Some other planets, like Mars, have more of the poisonous gas carbon dioxide than the Earth does.

- All living things are made up, in some part, of the element carbon. This is formed when matter burns. Earth had this too, from its explosive birth. Early Earth was so hot that there were many volcanoes that threw up more carbon.

- The force of **gravity** keeps you in place. It also holds the Earth's atmosphere! Smaller planets like Mercury have no atmosphere.

- The temperature on Earth is suitable for life.

- Water supports life. In its natural form, it has no harmful chemicals so we can drink it and forms of life can swim in it.

The evolution

Early life is believed to have begun in the oceans as simple, single-cell organisms called Protista. Fungi and algae are Protists. As time went by and the Earth cooled, life spread across it. Living creatures also grew in size and became diverse (more different) from each other.

A green Earth makes a healthier environment.

DID YOU KNOW?

The part of Earth that has life on it is called the ecosphere.

WHAT'S ON THE EARTH?

Does the Earth look round to you? It is in fact a little flat at the top and the bottom. The outer crust of the Earth is not smooth. Instead, it has mountains and hills, valleys and plains.

Huge patchwork!

The solid part of the Earth, or the crust and the outer part of the mantle, is called the Lithosphere. The crust may look like one piece of rock and soil, but it is actually made up of 21 plates. These are constantly moving, hitting each other or slipping away. This is called the Continental Drift.

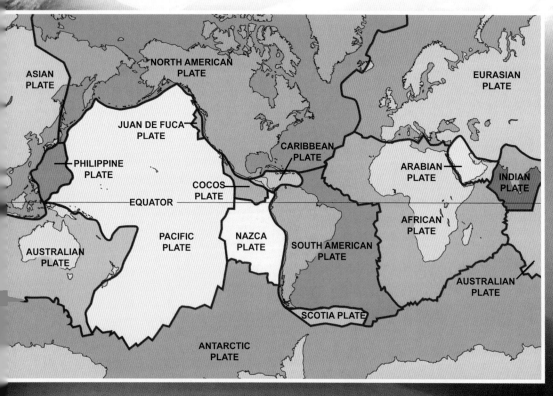

ASIAN PLATE

NORTH AMERICAN PLATE

JUAN DE FUCA PLATE

PHILIPPINE PLATE

COCOS PLATE

EQUATOR

CARIBBEAN PLATE

EURASIAN PLATE

ARABIAN PLATE

INDIAN PLATE

AFRICAN PLATE

AUSTRALIAN PLATE

PACIFIC PLATE

NAZCA PLATE

SOUTH AMERICAN PLATE

AUSTRALIAN PLATE

SCOTIA PLATE

ANTARCTIC PLATE

Always On The Move

The plates have been moving or drifting along for millions of years. Scientists believe the land mass was one piece and the continents have broken apart because of the continental drift. They believe North and South America broke away westwards from what is now the west coast of Europe and Africa.

Fun Facts

The continental crust under the mountains is the deepest on Earth. It runs to a depth of about 35 km (22 miles) under the Himalayan mountain range, making the thickest area of crust on Earth.

The Himalayan mountain range — including some of the highest peaks on Earth.

Different mountains

When there is a weak spot in the crust or the surface of the Earth (on land or under the sea), the hot, liquid magma below can gush out. These explosive mountains are called volcanoes. The liquid that pours out is called lava.

The Earth's moving plates hit each other with such huge force millions of years ago that they forced rock upwards to form mountains. These formations, like the Himalayas, are called Fold Mountains. When the tectonic plates move suddenly, we feel an **earthquake**.

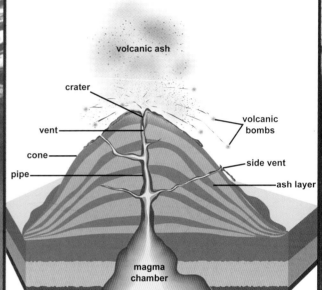

volcanic ash

crater

vent

cone

pipe

volcanic bombs

side vent

ash layer

magma chamber

- The Earth's crust covers less than one per cent of the planet's total volume.

- Lava can reach a temperature of nearly 1,200° Celsius!

- The Earth's plates move up to 10 cm (4 in) per year.

DID YOU KNOW?

Plate Tectonics is the study of the plates that make up the Earth's crust.

THE EARTH'S ATMOSPHERE

The Earth is surrounded by different gases that form the atmosphere. The atmosphere is a huge band of colourless gases, dust particles and water vapour that is about 483 km (300 miles) high.

Do we need it?

The atmosphere acts like a blanket, keeping out harmful ultraviolet rays from the Sun. The atmosphere allows the warmth of the Sun to touch the Earth. But it also keeps some of this warmth trapped so that the Earth stays warm enough to support life. The gases in the atmosphere make up the air that we breathe.

How did they get there?

The atmosphere was formed when gases like carbon dioxide, nitrogen, sulphur dioxide and water vapour were let out from inside the Earth. There is no exact point where the atmosphere ends. It just gets thinner and lighter and blends into outer space.

Fun Facts

If you went soaring through the atmosphere in a hot air balloon, you would find it harder to breathe the higher you went as the atmosphere got thinner.

Layered like an onion

Exosphere: outermost layer of the Earth's atmosphere. Stretches from about 644 km (400 miles) to about 1,287 km (800 miles) high.

Ionosphere: stretches from about 69-80 km (43-50 miles) to about 644 km (400 miles) away from the Earth.

Mesosphere: extends between 50 km (31 miles) to about 80 km (50 miles). The temperature falls quickly the higher you go.

Stratosphere: the belt between 18 km (11 miles) and 50 km (31 miles) above the Earth. This is where the ozone layer is. The ozone layer absorbs harmful rays from the Sun. You'd find high clouds in the lower stratosphere.

Troposphere: the air band closest to Earth, stretching from the surface to about 18 km (11 miles) high. This is where you'd find clouds and weather. Warmest near the Earth, it cools as you travel up. Its upper boundary is called the tropopause.

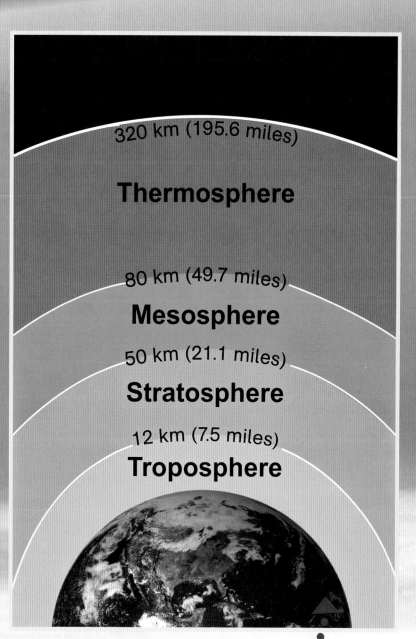

320 km (195.6 miles)

Thermosphere

80 km (49.7 miles)

Mesosphere

50 km (21.1 miles)

Stratosphere

12 km (7.5 miles)

Troposphere

The troposphere is where you find life on Earth.

IMPORTANCE OF WATER

How did water first appear on Earth? No one is sure. However, one thing is certain: water is essential to the survival of all living beings.

Where did water first come from?

Some scientists believe water (a chemical combination of hydrogen and oxygen denoted by the formula H_2O) formed when the Earth was cooling down and trapped gases were released. Others believe oceans formed when asteroids containing water hit Earth. Still others believe chemical compounds broke down and formed water. Water contains dissolved minerals and gases.

Glaciers and icebergs are frozen water.

The significance of water

Any form of life on Earth relies on water and we need water for almost all our bodily functions: the blood that flows through the body is part water; food cannot be swallowed or digested without water; plants need water to draw up dissolved minerals from the soil; without water, they cannot make their food through **photosynthesis**.

photosynthesis

sunlight

sugars

oxygen

carbon dioxide

water

- Water goes around in the water cycle: water vapour gets together to form clouds that drop as rain, snow, hail or sleet. This water fills oceans, caps glaciers or runs underground.
- Plants transpire (breathe out water vapour). Sunlight evaporates water, turning it into gaseous water vapour.
- The droplets of water vapour form clouds once again!

That's all water!

Water can be in three states: solid ice, liquid or invisible gas or water vapour that forms clouds. Water covers over 70 per cent of the Earth, filling different water bodies. Less than 3 per cent is frozen in glaciers and in ice in the Polar regions.

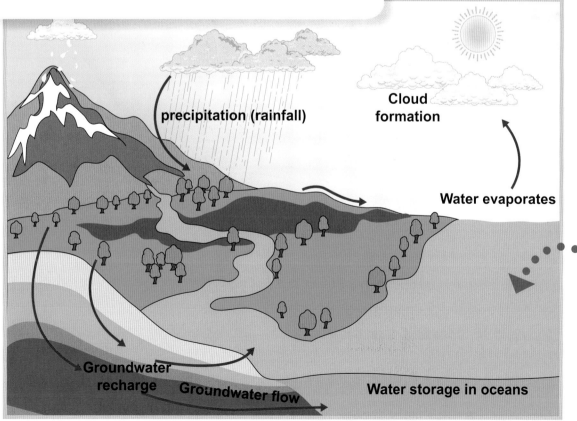

precipitation (rainfall)

Cloud formation

Water evaporates

Groundwater recharge

Groundwater flow

Water storage in oceans

The water cycle — it would be impossible to live without this phenomenon.

LIVING CONDITIONS

All the natural conditions that affect us make weather: the amount of sunshine; wind direction and its force; precipitation like rain, snow, hail or sleet; the clouds; and even visibility, or how far you can see, all make up the weather.

What's climate?

The weather over a long period of time is called climate. The climate of an area is determined by its altitude, its distance from the **Equator** and even by mountain ranges and oceans nearby. When weatherpeople speak of the climate of a place, they take into account up to 30 years of weather data.

Different seasons

The four major seasons are spring, summer, autumn and winter.

Because the Earth's axis is tilted towards the Sun, the northern and southern halves (or **hemispheres**) enjoy opposite seasons, depending on which hemisphere is closer to the Sun during orbit.

The four seasons — each different from the other.

Now it's sunny, now it's not

A noticeable change in weather over some months is called a season. Seasons change as the Earth revolves around the Sun and the tilt of the Earth's **axis** moves a hemisphere closer to/ further away from the Sun. This alters the amount of light a place gets and creates the weather typical of the seasons.

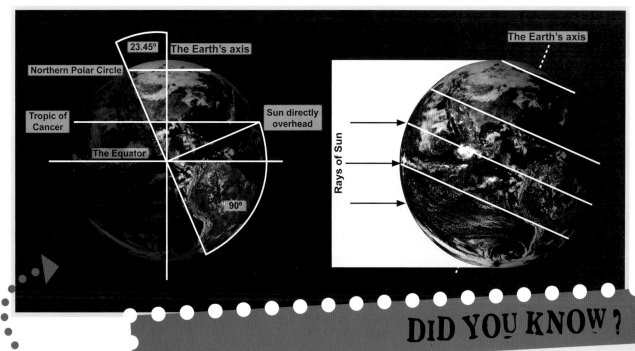

23.45° The Earth's axis

Northern Polar Circle

Tropic of Cancer

The Equator

Sun directly overhead

90°

The Earth's axis

Rays of Sun

The summer solstice (left) and the winter solstice (right).

DID YOU KNOW?

North of the Northern Polar Circle the Sun shines for 24 hours a day in the height of summer and it is dark for 24 hours a day in winter.

THE EARTH'S HABITATS

Different animals and insects live in different places. Their homes are known as habitats. A place can become a habitat only when it has enough food, water and safety for living things to survive.

That's where I live!

Most creatures choose one habitat. The snow leopard, for example, is comfortable in the icy heights of mountains. It can survive in the cold because of an unusually thick coat. Its ears and body are smaller in size than a regular leopard, which helps reduce heat loss.

A snow leopard is perfectly suited to the cold environment.

Different homes

The biosphere is a term that relates to the areas on Earth where there is life. Oceans, lakes, rivers and seas are the hydrosphere. The region under the Earth's surface is called the lithosphere. Each habitat is different. Deserts have sand, rocks and very little water. Mountains have snow, rocks, slopes and barren terrain.

Diverse animal habitats

The Polar regions, at the northern and southernmost tips of the Earth, are covered in snow. They are home to Polar bears, penguins and seals. Whales, sharks, fish and water plants inhabit the oceans. The desert is home to plants like the cactus and animals like the camel. Frogs, beavers, otters and birds like the egret inhabit the wet marshes. In the rainforests you can find many different species of birds, animals, insects and reptiles.

The magnificent sea turtle.

Fun Facts

An ideal habitat has enough space, food and water. If too many animals jostle for space, some have to leave or will die because there's too much competition for food.

DID YOU KNOW ?

In 1929 a Russian scientist named Vladimir Vernadsky thought of the word biosphere to describe different zones on Earth.

INVERTEBRATES ON EARTH

Animals that do not have a backbone or spine are called invertebrates. Most animals are invertebrates. Only about 2 per cent of animals have a vertebra or spine.

Snails rely on touch and smell when they are hunting for food.

Soft but tough

Molluscs make up one of the largest groups of invertebrates. There are over 93,000 species of them. Some, such as snails, live on land and in water. Others, like the octopus, live in water alone.

Different invertebrates

Flatworms are a group of invertebrates that have soft bodies. Some of them, like tapeworms, live in the digestive system of animals, including humans. Arthropods are a group of invertebrates that have jointed legs. These include insects, arachnids or spiders, and crustaceans or shelled creatures like crabs.

- An earthworm can live on even if it loses a small part of its body.
- Most sponges are sessile, meaning they are fixed in one place.
- Molluscs often use the same organ for **excretion** and **reproduction**.

Because they are small, spiders have many natural predators.

Invertebrates of the sea

Jellyfish and corals belong to the same family of Cnidaria (pronounced nidaria) that have a jelly-like body. Sea urchins and sea cucumbers belong to the Echinodermata family. Like many other echinoderms, starfish move and feed with hundreds of tube feet on the underside of the body. They even have two stomachs.

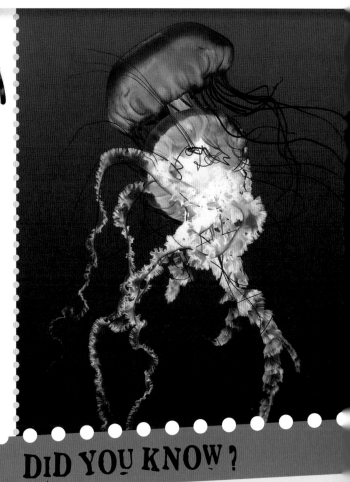

DID YOU KNOW?

Octopusses are considered the most intelligent invertebrates and can solve complex tasks during scientific experiments.

EARTH'S ANIMALS

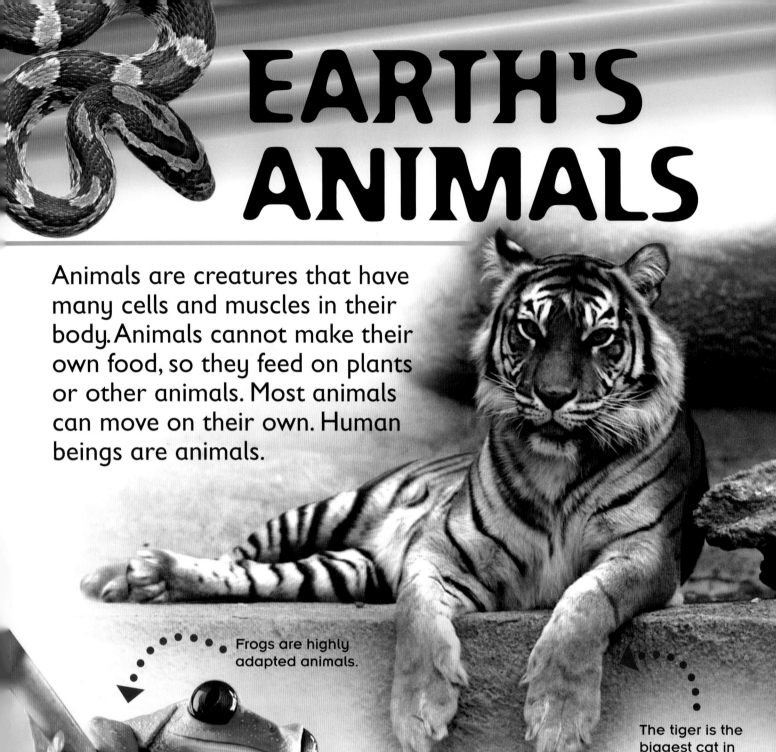

Animals are creatures that have many cells and muscles in their body. Animals cannot make their own food, so they feed on plants or other animals. Most animals can move on their own. Human beings are animals.

Frogs are highly adapted animals.

The tiger is the biggest cat in the world.

On land and in water

Some animals, like humans, dogs and tigers, live on land. Some, like fish and whales, live only in water. There are some animals, like frogs, salamanders and toads that live both on land and in water. These animals are called amphibians. They are cold-blooded creatures. Since they are cold-blooded creatures, amphibians have to hibernate, or go into a long winter sleep, when the temperature drops.

Blood runs cold...

Reptiles like snakes, lizards, alligators and turtles are cold-blooded. Reptiles have scaly skin and most of them lay eggs. The king cobra makes a nest to lay its eggs in. Some snakes like the boa constrictor and the green anaconda give birth to live young.

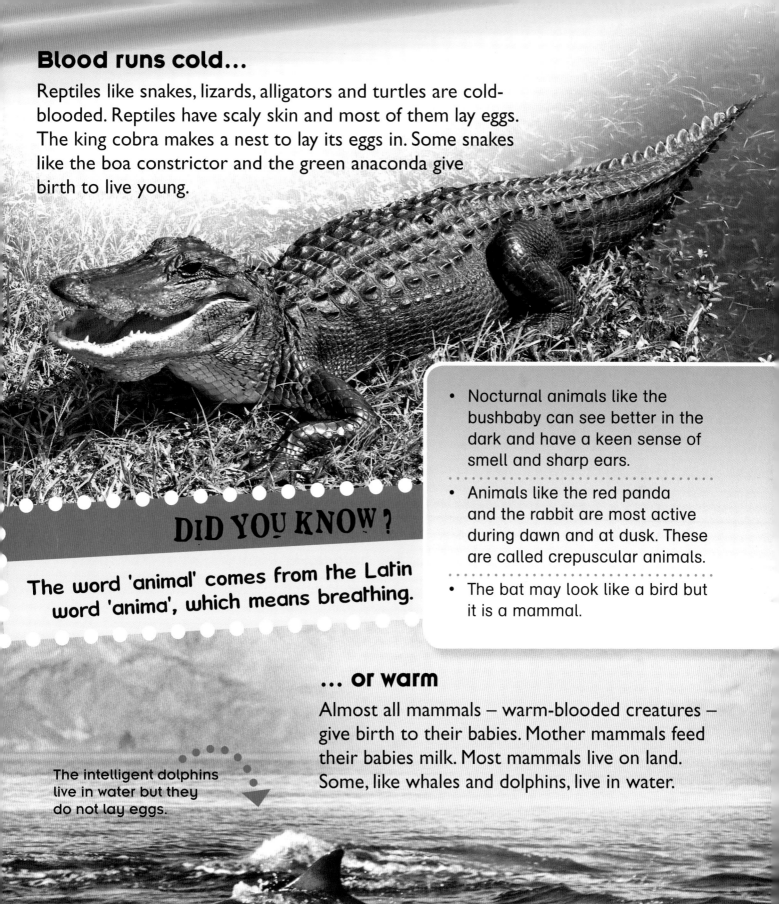

DID YOU KNOW ?

The word 'animal' comes from the Latin word 'anima', which means breathing.

- Nocturnal animals like the bushbaby can see better in the dark and have a keen sense of smell and sharp ears.
- Animals like the red panda and the rabbit are most active during dawn and at dusk. These are called crepuscular animals.
- The bat may look like a bird but it is a mammal.

... or warm

Almost all mammals – warm-blooded creatures – give birth to their babies. Mother mammals feed their babies milk. Most mammals live on land. Some, like whales and dolphins, live in water.

The intelligent dolphins live in water but they do not lay eggs.

BIRDS

A bird is a warm-blooded, two-legged creature that has a skeleton, beak and feathers. The front two legs have evolved into wings.

Flying high

Most birds can fly. Although they do walk or hop short distances, flying birds are helped by hollow bones that are light but strong. They have a strong breathing system that also helps them fly.

Strutting smart

Some birds cannot fly. Many of these birds are found on islands where they have fewer enemies. Some, like the ratites (including the ostrich, emu and cassowary), defend themselves with their sharp claws. Scientists believe that birds may have learnt to fly to escape to safety.

The eagle hunts small birds and animals.

For how long will they be around?

Fun Facts

There are more flightless birds on the island of New Zealand than anywhere else. These include the kiwi, takahe and penguin.

Swimming away

Birds like penguins and ducks can dive and swim underwater. Their shorter wings help them paddle. Underwater swimmers like grebes, loons and penguins have heavier bones than birds that fly. This helps them stay underwater. Other swimmers and divers like pelicans and terns are also good flyers.

Penguins are birds that can actually swim very well.

This little bird may have evolved from a dinosaur!

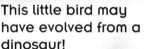

- Common loons are among the deepest divings birds, descending up to 153 m (500 ft)!

- The ostrich is the largest bird. It stands about 2.7 m high.

- The bee hummingbird lays the smallest egg among birds. Each egg is about the size of a pea! The ostrich lays the largest bird egg. It weighs over 1.3 kg (3 lbs).

- Hummingbirds are some of the best hoverers. They can stay in one place for some time, beating their wings about 52 times a second.

DID YOU KNOW?

Some birds, like the flightless dodo, have become extinct. This bird was last seen on the island of Mauritius in the late 17th century.

THE INSECT WORLD

Insects are a class of creatures called arthropods. There are over a million insects that we know of. This makes them the most varied and numerous of all living creatures.

What-a-pod?

Arthropods have jointed legs and insects have three pairs of those. They do not have a backbone. Instead, they have a hard outer body, or exoskeleton. You'd recognise an insect from its body, which is divided into three parts: the head, thorax and abdomen. Indeed, the word 'insect' means 'sections' in Latin.

Fun Facts

Among the arthropods, insects are the biggest group. They are also the only arthropods with wings.

Different insects

The praying mantis eats other insects. This makes it a friend of the gardener, since it eats up aphids and moths that eat plants. It gets its name from the way it catches its food – remaining motionless with its forelegs pressed together. Like many other insects, it can **camouflage** itself among plants as it waits for prey. This strange insect can move its head almost all the way around!

The praying mantis is an accomplished hunter!

The common fly is a pest that spreads disease.

Insects and diseases

Some insects can spread illness. There are more than 2,500 species of mosquito and they spread malaria, dengue, encephalitis, yellow fever and many other diseases. The fly spreads disease like cholera, dysentery and typhoid that it transports on its legs after landing on waste matter.

DID YOU KNOW?

You find more insects the warmer the climate. This means the number of insects decreases as you move from the Equator towards the Poles.

LIFE IN THE WATERS

The first life on Earth began in the sea. Ocean life is diverse. It can be home to microscopic zooplankton or enormous whales.

Spineless creature!

Some creatures of the sea don't have a spine. These invertebrates include jellyfish, anemones, molluscs such as squids and octopusses, and spiny creatures or echinodermata like the sea urchin.

Making bones about it

Fish are among the most common sea creatures, although they also enjoy living in fresh waters. Some, like the hilsa, live in the sea and swim up the river to lay eggs. One of the tiniest fish is the stout infantfish, which is less than half an inch long. At the other end of the scale are sharks. The whale shark is the largest fish and can grow to almost 12 m (40 ft) long. Mammals such as whales also live in the seas. The blue whale is the largest living animal.

DID YOU KNOW?

Not all fish are safe to eat. The pufferfish has a poison that can paralyse a human.

- Copepods are tiny shrimp-like creatures that are the favourite food of many creatures of the sea.
- The clownfish is one of the few creatures that can live among poisonous anemones.
- The coelacanth has been around for millions of years.
- The cookiecutter shark takes a round bite of its prey's flesh – hence the name.
- Seals and walruses live on land and in the sea.

PLANT LIFE ON EARTH

Plants are living creatures. They can be as large as trees and as tiny as algae. There are over 287,655 species of plants.

That's old!

The plant world also includes shrubs and bushes, ferns, mosses, fungi and even some algae. Land plants appeared on Earth around 700 million years ago. As more plants began to grow, they used up more carbon dioxide to make their food by photosynthesis. They also gave out more oxygen, which was necessary for animals to survive.

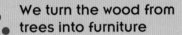

We turn the wood from trees into furniture

Thank you plants!

Everything we eat comes from, or relies upon, plants. Sometimes it's indirect, when the animals we eat in turn feed on plants. We eat the seeds of plants like rice and wheat. The roots of potatoes, carrots and radishes make nutritious vegetables. Spices like pepper that flavour our food come from plants.

What's that?

Almost all plants begin from a seed, although some, like ferns, are born from spores. The roots hold the plant firmly to the ground. They also draw up water and dissolved minerals that the plant uses to make food. The stems hold the leaves, flowers and fruit – the seed of the plant. When the seed falls to the ground, it begins to grow into a new plant.

He's actually chewing a plant.

Fun Facts

Chewing gum is made of chicle, a natural gum from the Manilkara chicle tree that grows in America.

DID YOU KNOW?

The study of the uses of plants is known as ethnobotany.

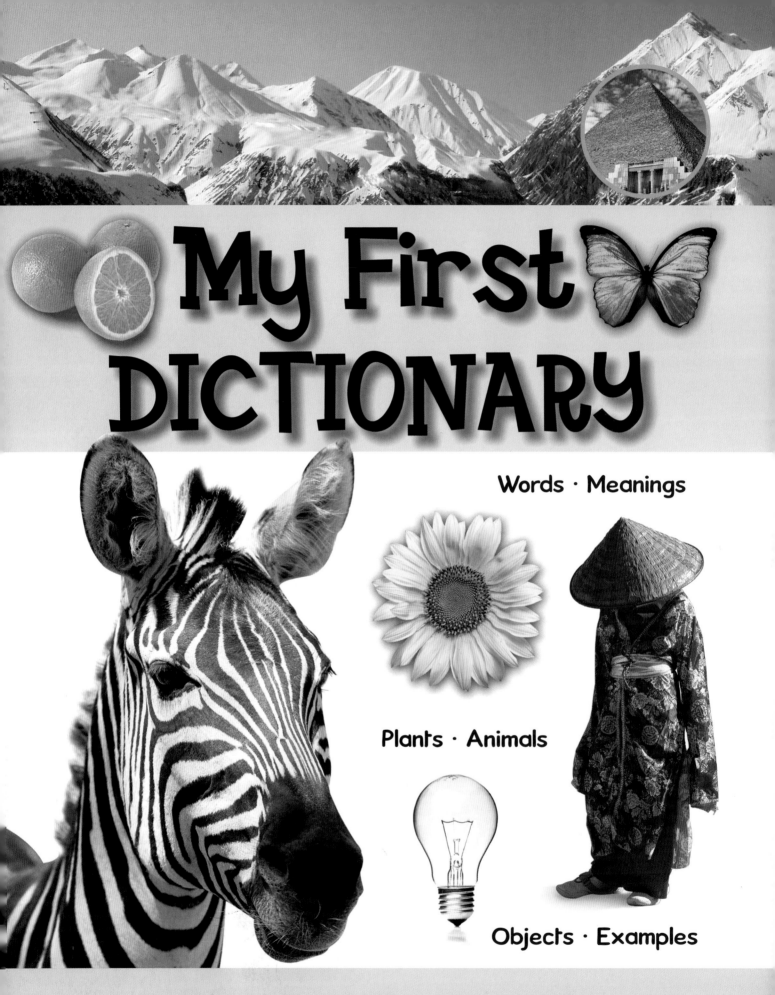

My First DICTIONARY

Words · Meanings

Plants · Animals

Objects · Examples

A fun reference book of first words

A

above
up or higher

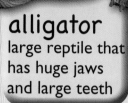

alligator
large reptile that has huge jaws and large teeth

art
art can be anything, including a painting, sculpture, drawing, music, photograph, or any other form of expression

astronaut
person whose job is to explore space

awake
state of not being asleep

award
something you get for doing well

awash
state of being covered with water

academy
institution for the advancement of knowledge

act
to do something or perform a role

addition
adding of numbers to get a sum

address
an address states where someone lives or works

aeroplane
flying vehicle with fixed wings and an engine

adjective
word that describes a place, thing or person

adult
grown up man or woman

adverb
an adverb states 'how', 'when', 'where', or 'how much'. Examples include *quickly, easily, mainly*, etc.

afraid
state of being frightened or scared

alike
when two or more objects are similar, they're alike

anatomy
science of the body

ant
small, social insects

ambulance
vehicle that takes sick or injured people to the hospital

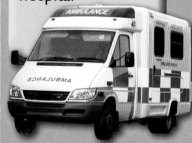

ape
large tailless primate

arm
part of the human body between the shoulder and the elbow

arrows
long, thin objects with a sharp point

axe
sharp metal tool used to chop wood

B

batter
uncooked, liquid mixture of eggs, flour, butter and other ingredients. Cakes, cookies and muffins are made from batter

baboon
large monkey with large cheek pouches and a big snout

baby
very young child

banana
sweet, yellow fruit

barn
farm building where animals and their food are kept

beads
small objects with a hole through them. Used to make jewellery

book
composition of words that has been published

bear
big, furry animal

brush
object used to clean, paint or groom

bulb
turns electricity into light

burrow
tunnel or hole dug by a small animal

bagel
bread roll shaped like a doughnut

blast
sudden and very loud noise

brain
organ that helps us to think. The brain is protected by the skull

brave
someone who is not afraid to face dangerous situations

broken
state of something that has been separated into two or more pieces

broom
object used to sweep the floor

bus
large road vehicle that transports people

a **b** c d e f g h i j k l m

cab
another name for a taxi

cabbage
leafy plant eaten as a vegetable

cake
sweet dessert

can
container that stores food and drink

candle
stick made of wax that has a wick

cap
type of hat

cast
throw forcefully

chair
piece of furniture that people can sit on

cabin
simple house usually made of wood

camel
large mammal that lives in desert areas

chart
diagram that shows the relationship between things

chimney
structure that funnels smoke away from a fire

chisel
tool with flat blade and sharp edge

circle
round figure where all points are an equal distance from the centre

cliff
steep structure of soil and rock

cone
shape that has a point at one end and a circular opening at the other

cry
to shed tears from the eyes

courage
quality to face danger or pain without showing too much fear

crawl
moving with body near the ground

cub
the young of certain animals, such as lions and bears

cube
geometric figure with six square sides

curtains
material hung to provide a covering or screen

couple
two similar objects in a pair or two people

crane
long-necked bird that lives in wet areas

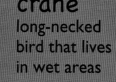

D

dirty
opposite of clean

dog
pet animals commonly kept by humans

dad
another word for father

dark
opposite of light

deer
long-legged mammals that have hooved feet

daughter
female child

December
last month of the year

desert
very dry area

diamond
very hard, shiny jewel

dollar
currency used in many countries

doll
a small figure kept as a toy

dolphin
marine mammal with teeth and a long nose

door
entrance to a house or room

down
opposite of up

drain
a channel or pipe that carries liquid away

dress
piece of clothing with a top and a skirt

drill
to make a hole

drop
to let something fall

doctor
person who says what's wrong with you when you're ill

duck
bird that swims well and lives near the water

dusk
time of day after sunset

drum
musical instrument

a b c d e f g h i j k l m

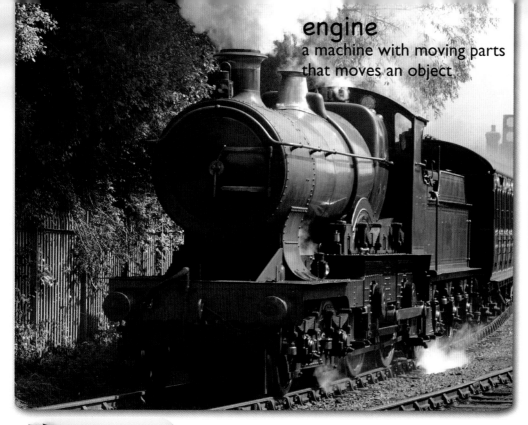

engine
a machine with moving parts that moves an object

E

Europe
continent in the Northern Hemisphere, including the UK, Ireland, Italy, Germany, France and Spain

egg
an oval or round object laid by most non-mammal female creatures

emperor
ruler of a country

excellent
very good; outstanding

empty
containing nothing

elbow
joint in the middle of the arm

entrance
an opening

eagle
large bird of prey with a hooked beak and sharp talons

eleven
ten plus one

envelope
folded paper or card to contain letters and other items

eraser
object used to rub off pencil marks

eager
having or showing keen interest or desire

exercise
physical or mental exertion that is done to improve health and performance

earn
to receive something for working

elephant
largest land animal, with a long trunk

extinct
to have died-out as a species. Extinct animals include dodos and dinosaurs

F

fast
ability to act or move quickly

fawn
young deer

fear
to be afraid or scared

femur
upper leg bone, which is the longest in the human body

fin
fish have fins that help them swim

flag
square or rectangular piece of material that represents a country, state, province, or city

flower
the part of the plant containing the organs that make new plants, usually surrounded by petals

firefighter
person who puts out fires and saves lives

fork
object with prongs used for eating solid food

fraction
part of a whole. Half of an orange is a fraction of an orange

funnel
conical shaped structure with a wide opening at one end and a narrow opening at the other

furniture
tables, beds and chairs are all furniture

furrow
a long narrow trench in the ground for planting seeds or helping water drain

fruit
part of some plants that contain seeds. Apples and oranges are fruits

face
front of the head carrying features such as the mouth and nose

factory
a building where things are made or put together

falcon
bird of prey that hunts other birds and small animals

family
group of people who are related to each other

famous
very well known

farmer
person who looks after animals and produces food by growing plants

foal
young horse

future
time that is yet to come

garden
man-made area where plants and flowers grow

gate
a hinged barrier in a fence

gather
to collect

gazelle
a small slender antelope found in Africa and Asia

geography
study of the location of people and features on earth

geyser
natural hot spring that sprays steam and water above the ground

gibe
make fun of

giddy
condition of having a dizzying sensation

give
when you let someone have something, you 'give' the person that thing

glasses
objects used to help people see more clearly

glue
substance that sticks things together

gibbon
small, tree-dwelling ape found in Asia

gnat
small flying insect

gold
precious metal. Some coins and jewellery are made of gold

golf
sport where a ball is hit into a series of holes using metal sticks called clubs

grandparents
the mother and father of each of your parents

gift
something you give someone without asking anything in return

guitar
musical instrument, usually with six or 12 strings and a fingerboard with frets to create different chords

G

grass
common plant that forms a green covering over the ground

grate
to make into very small shreds

guest
visitor to a house

H

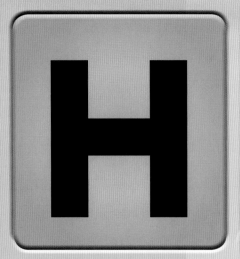

haystack
big pile of hay

habitat
natural place where animals and plants live

hail
pellets of frozen rain that fall from clouds

ham
meat from a pig's leg that is salted and dried or smoked

harp
musical instrument with many strings

hat
a shaped covering, worn on the head

hatchet
axe with a short handle

heart
an organ made of muscle that pumps blood around the body

hem
a sewn edge of a piece of material

herbivore
plant-eating animal

hero
person with courage and character who is known for their good deeds

hoe
garden tool with a long handle and flat blade

hoof
hard, protective covering on the feet of some animals. Deer, zebras and horses have hooves

hornet
wasp-like flying insect capable of stinging

honey
a sweet, sticky liquid made by bees from nectar

hound
a dog bred to track animals by scent

hurricane
dangerous storm with fast winds and heavy rainfall

hyena
meat-eating animal that hunts and scavenges prey

hamster
small rodent sometimes kept as a pet

hose
flexible pipe through which water flows, usually used to water plants

I

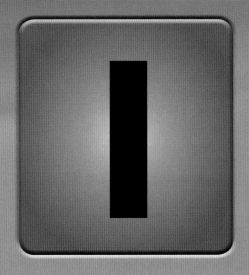

iceberg
a large floating mass of ice that has separated from an ice sheet

icicle
hanging ice that forms when dripping water freezes over time

igloo
house made from blocks of ice

impala
a graceful antelope found in large herds in southern Africa

infant
a very young child or baby

irate
feeling or showing great anger

island
piece of land surrounded by water

J

jacket
short coat

janitor
someone who cleans a building

n o p q r s t u v w x y z

K

jab
poke abruptly

jet
fast and
powerful aeroplane

jewel
precious stone

judo
a form of martial arts

junk
traditional Chinese
sailing ship build
from wood

justice
when something
is treated fairly
and reasonably

kangaroo
a large marsupial
with powerful
back legs found
in Australia

kayak
small, narrow boat

kennel
shelter for dogs

kidney
bean-shaped organs
in the human
body that helps to
produce urine

kilt
traditional dress
worn by the people
of Scotland

kiwi
flightless bird found
in New Zealand

knee
part of the
body where
the leg bends

label
paper or fabric attached to an item that gives information

lace
delicate fabric

ladle
large spoon used to serve gravy and soup

lemonade
drink made from lemons, water and sugar

laundry
clothing that is about to be washed or has just been washed

lava
molten rock that erupts from volcanoes

lawn
an area covered with short grass that is maintained

lake
large body of water surrounded by land

lane
narrow road in a rural area

lever
a rigid bar attached to a pivot, used to help move things

library
a building or room containing books and other material that you can use and borrow

lifeboat
a small boat used to evacuate a larger ship; a boat launched from land to save people in trouble at sea

link
a relationship between two things

log
short piece of a tree trunk or branch

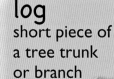

liquid
one of the three forms of matter, with gasses and solids being the others. Water is a liquid

lobster
a large marine crustacean with claws

lunch
meal eaten in the middle of the day

lungs
organs through which animals breathe

lamb
baby sheep

n   o   p   q   r   s   t   u   v   w   x   y   z

M

macaroni
narrow tubes of pasta

magician
An artist who performs magic is known as a magician. Magic is the art of performing illusions and tricks

magnifying glass
lens that can make things look bigger than their actual size

mailbox
box where letters are put

mammal
typically any warm-blooded animal with hair or fur. Mammals nourish their young with milk

mammoth
large, elephant-like animal of the Ice Ages

marsh
wet and grassy land

marsupial
mammals with pouches, where the young are kept. Kangaroos and koalas are marsupials

meal
good amount of food eaten at one time

medal
award given for a good performance

metal
shiny, solid element that can conduct heat and electricity. Gold, copper, silver and iron are metals

mountain

natural elevation from the earth's surface that is higher than a hill

mittens

thick gloves that keep the hands warm

mole

burrowing mammal with powerful claws and poor eyesight

mosaic

work of art made up of pieces of glass, tiles, stones, or other objects fitted together

moth

nocturnal flying insect related to butterflies

muffin

small cake

mummy

preserved dead body usually related to Ancient Egypt

museum

a building where objects of interest are displayed

n o p q r s t u v w x y z

N

nest
structure made of twigs where birds lay eggs and take care of their young

nail
hard surface that grows at the end of the fingers and toes

nag
bother or worry persistently

nanny
person employed to care for a child in their own home

napkin
something with which you clean your face after eating

narrow
not very wide, usually in relation to an object's length or height

nap
short sleep during the day

neat
clean and proper

neighbour
someone living close to your house

neon
gas that is used in some lights

new
condition of something that has never been used before

newspaper
printed publication that gives information about current events of public interest

newt
bright-coloured amphibian

nib
the pointed end part of a pen

nightingale
bird that is known for singing beautiful songs

nocturnal
condition of being more active at night than the daytime. Bats are nocturnal creatures

nod
the up and down movement of the head

note
short written message

noun
word that represents a person, place or thing

nut
fruit with a hard shell

nurse
person that looks after you when you are sick

noodles
strips of pasta or similar dough, typically made with eggs

nutmeg
seed of a tropical tree that is used as a spice

a b c d e f g h i j k l m

oar
tool generally made of wood that is used to row a boat

observatory
place from where people observe the skies, using tools such as telescopes

ocean
a very large expanse of sea

oil
a thick, sticky liquid made from petrol

Olympics
the Olympic games began in ancient Greece over 2,700 years ago. The games are held every four years

octopus
creature that has eight arms covered in suction cups

olive
small oval fruit

omnivore
animal that eats both plants and meat. Humans are omnivores

omit
to leave out

orbit
fixed path that one object takes to circle around another. The moon orbits the earth, and the earth orbits the sun

orca
a large toothed member of the dolphin family with black and white markings

ostrich
largest bird in the world

otter
playful aquatic mammal

ounce
unit of weight that is one-twelfth of a pound

oval
rounded egg shape

oven
an enclosed compartment used for cooking food

ox
another name for a cow or bull

orchid
colourful flower that grows in warm areas

oyster
soft-bodied mollusk with a hard protective shell often eaten raw as a delicacy

ozone
colourless toxic gas that forms a protective layer from the sun in our atmosphere

overcoat
long warm coat worn over clothing

P

pebble
small, smooth stone

package
object or objects, placed in a box or wrapped for transport

paddle
a short oar used for rowing a small boat

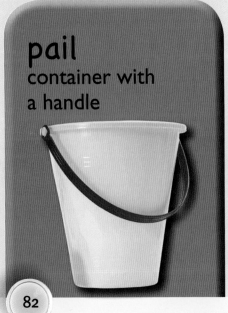

pail
container with a handle

palette
thin board, on which an artist mixes paint

party
social gathering of invited guests

pentagon
five-sided shape

pepper
spice people use on their food

pod
group of whales

pupil
person who is learning in an educational institution

proverb
short saying that is a commonly known truth

puppet
small doll that is made to move by pulling strings

puzzle
game that requires logic and knowledge to solve it

qualm
feeling of doubt and uneasiness

quack
the sound of a duck

quarter
the portion of something when divided equally into four; coin worth 25 American cents

quicksand
loose, wet sand where objects can sink

quiet
calm or without noise

quilt
a warm bed covering made of padding between layers of fabric stitched together

quip
to make a joke or a witty remark

quit
give up; go away or leave

quiver
container where arrows are kept

quiz
a test of knowledge

R

rake
garden tool that helps to collect leaves and grass

rabbit
small mammal with big ears

racket
loud and disturbing noise

radar
device that is used to locate objects at a distance

radio
communication device where you can listen to music and talk shows

radius
distance from the centre of a circle to the border

raisin
dried grape

rattle
series of short, rapid knocking sounds

recipe
set of instructions for making a particular dish, usually of food

a b c d e f g h i j k l m

reef
a ridge of jagged rock, coral or sand just above or below the surface of the sea

refrigerator
machine that keeps food cold and fresh

rein
strap that a rider controls and steers a horse with

rhinoceros
large, thick-skinned animal with one or two horns on its head

rhyme
to have similar sounds, like 'kite' and 'light', 'bite' and 'right' etc.

robot
machine programmed to move automatically and perform specific functions

rocket
a tube filled with fuel that can be propelled to great heights

rodent
mammal whose two front teeth grow constantly. Mice, squirrels, hamsters, and rats are all rodents

roof
covering of a room or building

roost
to sit on a perch

rooster
male chicken

roots
plant parts below the ground that get water and other nutrients from the soil

route
the way or course taken to get to a destination

rug
floor covering made of thick fabric

S

scroll
a roll of parchment or paper for writing or painting on

shrub
low-lying bush with a woody stem

silk
delicate thread used to make fine fabric

sill
wood that forms the base of a window

sack
container made of fabric, paper or plastic that you can put things in

sail
large piece of strong fabric that catches wind and helps a boat move through the water

scallop
an edible mollusk with a ribbed, fan-shaped shell

seal
a device or substance that joins two items together

season
each of winter, spring, summer, and autumn that mark particular weather patterns and daylight hours

silo
a tower or pit used to store grain

skull
bony structure of the head that protects the brain

sleet
freezing rain

shovel
tool used to dig and move material

slither
to move smoothly and without obstruction

snail
a mollusk with a spiral shell that the whole body can be withdrawn into

steak
slice of meat or fish for grilling or frying

swap
to give something in exchange for something else

strait
narrow body of water connecting two bigger bodies of water

synthesizer
musical instrument that electronically creates sounds

snap
to break something in two, usually with a cracking sound

swamp
wet area that usually has a lot of animal and plant life

soil
the upper layer of earth in which plants grow

sphere
ball-shaped object

T

tablet
a flat slab of stone, clay or wood

tambourine
shallow drum with metal discs used as a percussion instrument

toddler
a young child just beginning to walk

telescope
instrument through which distant objects appear closer

tent
shelter made of fabric that can be moved

tie
narrow band of fabric that is tied around the neck

thunder
a loud rumbling or crashing sound heard after lightning due to rapidly expanding air

tongs
simple pincer tool used to pick things up

tornado
rapidly spinning air that is shaped like a funnel

town
urban area smaller than a city

tract
large area of land

a b c d e f g h i j k l m

tractor
powerful farm vehicle, usually with large treaded wheels

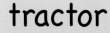

truce
state of peace between two opposing parties

trust
to be confident about and have faith in something

tub
large vessel for holding or storing liquids

tuck
to push, fold or turn something to hold it in place

tugboat
sturdy boat that guides other bigger boats in and out of harbours

trail
rough path

triangle
a shape with three straight sides

trunk
tree's major support

trout
a fish of the salmon family often fished for food

twister
another name for a tornado – rapidly spinning air that can be very dangerous

n o p q s (t) u v w x y z

U

ukulele
small four-stringed guitar with its origins in Hawaii

unicorn
mythical, one-horned animal

uniform
special outfit worn by members of one particular group

unite
combine or join

urban
located in or related to a city

urge
very strong desire

V

vase
a decorative container used for displaying flowers

utensils
tools used in the kitchen, like forks, knives and spoons

W

vat
large tub that is used to holds liquids

veteran
a person who has long experience in a particular field

vine
plant that does not have a support of its own and grows on other objects

vocabulary
group of words that a person knows and understands

vote
a formal choice someone gives between candidates or options

vowel
any of the letters a, e, i, o, and u

wagon
vehicle with wheels that is drawn by a tractor or animals

wand
thin rod that magicians carry

watch
small clock that you normally wear on the wrist

weary
state of being very tired

weasel
small, furry mammals having short legs

whisk
tool used to beat eggs or batter

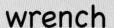

wrench
tool that is used to turn nuts or bolts

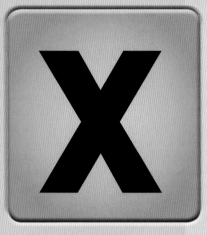

X

x-ray
special picture of your teeth or bones taken in a hospital or a dentists

xylophone
musical instrument with rows of bars

Y

yam
the American name for the sweet potato, a vegetable

yard
small area of land attached to a house

yardstick
a measuring stick equal to one yard, or three feet, in length

yarn
cord of twisted fibre that is used in weaving and sewing

yacht
a medium-sized boat with sails

yell
to shout in a loud voice

yak
large wild ox with shaggy hair, humped shoulders and large horns

yolk
yellow portion of an egg

yelp
bark in a high-pitched tone

yore
something of a long time ago

Z

zebra
horse-like animal with black and white stripes

zeal
great energy or enthusiasm in pursuit of a cause or objective

zero
no quantity or number; naught

zigzag
line or course with abrupt left and right turns

zip
two strips of metal or plastic that are joined together with a slider

zoologist
scientist who studies animals

My First ATLAS

Minerals

Monuments

Places

Resources

Maps

People

A visual guide to the countries of the world

CANADA AND THE USA

Canada is geographically bigger than the United States, but the latter is nine times more populated.

ALASKA (USA)

The 'inunnguaq' represents a human figure.

CANADA
Capital: Ottawa
Area: 9.09 million sq/km
Climate: temperate to extreme cold
Population: 33 million

Canada

Canada is the second largest country in the world and shares land borders with the United States to the south and the northwest. It has a small population and the **landscape** is frozen most of the year. It was first inhabited by aboriginal people and later by the British and French.

Edmonton

Winnipeg

The CN Tower in Toronto is one of the tallest buildings in the world.

Ottawa

Toronto

United States of America

The United States of America is a huge country with 50 states. The country is situated mostly in central North America, with Washington, D.C. as its capital. The United States lies between the Pacific and Atlantic Oceans, bordered by Canada to the north and Mexico to the south. The country is regarded as the most powerful nation in the world with lots of **natural resources.**

The Statue of Liberty in New York was gifted to the US by France.

Seattle

United States of America
Capital: Washington, D.C.
Area: 9.16 million sq/km
Climate: mostly temperate
Population: 307 million

Denver

Los Angeles

Dallas

Chicago

Washington, D.C.

Alaska

Alaska is the country's biggest state, but also the least dense in terms of population. It once belonged to Russia, before the US purchased it in 1867 for $7.2 million!

Fun Facts

The venus fly trap only lives in the wild in the Carolinas and nowhere else in the world.

DID YOU KNOW?

Basketball was invented by a Canadian named Dr. James Naismith. He invented the game while working in Boston with college students.

MEXICO AND CENTRAL AMERICA

Mexico and Central America form a natural bridge linking the United States with South America. The culturally rich region is full of ancient, historical ruins.

Mexico

Mexico is famous for its culture, especially the largely untouched ruins of the Mayan civilisation. This country of over 100 million is full of natural splendour — from the lovely plains and mountains to its beautiful coastline.

MEXICO
Capital: Mexico City
Area: 1.92 million sq/km
Climate: tropical to desert
Population: 111 million

Fun Facts

Mexico City hosted the nineteenth Olympic Games in 1968. It is the only Latin America country to do so. It has also hosted the FIFA World Cup twice, in 1970 and 1986.

Nicaragua

Nicaragua is the largest Central American country. Its history is tainted by civil wars, and volcanoes and earthquakes are always a threat to this country. However, it has its share of natural attractions. The coral reefs and the mangrove forests are rich with flora and fauna, and are a big hit with tourists.

Belize

Belize is located on the Caribbean coast of Central America. The landscape is sprinkled with Maya ruins and **diverse** animal life, ranging from the jaguar to the toucan monkey. Belize also has the Western Hemisphere's longest coral reef.

Chichen Itza in Mexico — remains of the mighty Maya civilisation.

○ Mexico City

Guatemala City ●

Belmopan

Managua ●

Since 1828, the Poas volcano in Costa Rica has erupted 39 times.

San Jose ●

Costa Rica

Costa Rica is located between the Pacific Ocean and the Caribbean Sea. Its picturesque landscape makes this small country an ideal tourist destination. Costa Rica literally translates as 'rich coast' and the country is known for its coffee production.

BELIZE
Capital: Belmopan
Area: 22,806 sq/km
Climate: tropical
Population: 307,000

COSTA RICA
Capital: San Jose
Area: 50,660 sq/km
Climate: tropical and subtropical
Population: 4.2 million

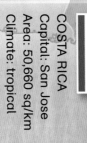

NORTH ANDEAN COUNTRIES

North Andean countries include Ecuador, Bolivia, Peru and Colombia.

Colombia

Colombia is the only country to touch both the Atlantic and the Pacific oceans. Colombia is famous for its jewellery, especially its emeralds. It is also known for having the continent's highest coal production. The climate is tropical because of its proximity to the equator, but there are peaks that are covered in snow owing to the altitude.

COLOMBIA
Capital: Bogota
Area: 1.03 million sq/km
Climate: tropical to cool
Population: 45 million

Ecuador

Ecuador is located on the northwestern corner of the South American continent. It has Colombia to its north, and Peru to the southeast. The Galapagos Islands are a part of Ecuador, and the country has some of the greatest **biodiversity** of any country in the world. The climate is mostly tropical, with an extreme rainy season.

ECUADOR
Capital: Quito
Area: 276,840 sq/km
Climate: mostly tropical
Population: 14.5 million

The Andes

The Andes mountain range dominates the west of the South American continent and is one of the longest mountain ranges in the world. It is over 7,000 km (4,400 miles) long, and 700 km (300 miles) at its widest. The average height of its mountains is about 4000 m (13,000 ft).

Fun Facts

The Galapagos volcanoes, 960 km (597 miles) west of Ecuador, bring a lot of tourists to the country because of their unique and diverse flora and fauna.

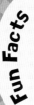

PERU
Capital: Lima
Area: 1.28 million sq/km
Climate: diverse (tropical to cool)
Population: 29 million

A colourful market in Otavolo, Ecuador.

The Machu Picchu ruins - remnants of a once-powerful Inca Empire.

Peru

Peru is the largest country in South America after Brazil and Argentina. It is unique for having three different landscapes – the rocky Andes, the Atacama Desert, and the Amazonian forest.

Bogota

Quito

Lima

BRAZIL AND NEIGHBOURING COUNTRIES

Brazil is South America's biggest country. Its neighbours include Argentina, Peru, Paraguay, Colombia, Venezuela, Suriname, Guyana, and Bolivia.

Guyana

Originally a Dutch colony in the 17th century, by 1815 Guyana had come under British rule. It is also one of the four non-Spanish-speaking territories on the continent, along with the states of Brazil (Portuguese) and Suriname (Dutch), and the French overseas region of French Guiana (French).

The Itaipu dam is the world's most powerful electricity generating station.

Trinidad and Tobago

The islands of Trinidad and Tobago may be close to each other, but have their own distinctive cultural flavours. Trinidad, mainly inhabited by people of African and Indian descent, is known for its steel music. Tobago, the smaller of the two islands, is slower paced and more scenic.

TRINIDAD AND TOBAGO
Capital: Port of Spain
Area: 5,128 sq km
Climate: tropical
Population: 1.2 million

VENEZUELA
Capital: Caracas
Area: 882,050 sq/km
Climate: tropical and moderate
Population: 27 million

GUYANA
Capital: Georgetown
Area: 196,850 sq/km
Climate: tropical
Population: 772,000

BRAZIL
Capital: Brasilia
Area: 8.45 million sq/km
Climate: mostly tropical
Population: 199 million

Caracas

Port of Spain

Georgetown

Paramaribo

Cayenne

Brasilia

Suriname

Suriname is home to the Maroons – descendants of African slaves who arrived about 300 years back. Its capital is Paramaribo.

Brazil

Brazil is the largest country in the continent occupying nearly half of South America. Brazil is also the fifth most populated country and the fourth most populated democracy in the world. Football is the national sport and is followed religiously.

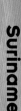

The Statue of Christ, Rio de Janeiro, Brazil.

Fun Facts

The Statue of Christ, the 130 ft tall statue that overlooks Rio de Janeiro, is one of the seven wonders of modern times. This sculpture is the symbol and icon of Brazil.

ARGENTINA AND NEIGHBOURING COUNTRIES

Argentina borders Paraguay and Bolivia to the north, Brazil and Uruguay to the northeast, and Chile to the west and south.

Argentina

Argentina is the second largest country in South America and eighth in the world. The country's culture is heavily shaped by the Europeans, most particularly the Italians and Spanish people, who formed the largest percentage of newcomers from 1860 to 1930.

The Atacama Desert dominates the Chilean landscape.

La Paz

La Paz, Bolivia, is the highest capital city in the world.

Fun Facts

Argentina's population is predominantly of European descent after a wave of European investment and immigration around 1870.

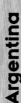

Chile

Chile is 4,000 km (2,485 miles) long and only 150 km (93 miles) wide on average. Eighty per cent of the country is covered by mountains. People are mostly of European descent or a mixture of European and indigenous ancestry. In the Atacama desert lie the Chuquicamata and Escondida copper mines.

CHILE
Capital: Santiago
Area: 748,800 sq/km
Climate: Diverse (temperate to cool and dry)
Population: 16.5 million

Santiago

Asuncion

PARAGUAY
Capital: Asuncion
Area: 397,300 sq/km
Climate: subtropical to temperate
Population: 7 million

Buenos Aires

Argentina is the birthplace of the graceful dance, tango.

ARGENTINA
Capital: Buenos Aires
Area: 2.73 million sq/km
Climate: mostly temperate
Population: 41 million

Montevideo

Uruguay

Uruguay is located in the southeastern part of the continent and is typified by low grasslands. It has the highest literacy rate and the lowest poverty rate in the continent and education is compulsory and free. The economy of the country is dominated by agriculture.

URUGUAY
Capital: Montevideo
Area: 173,620 sq/km
Climate: warm, temperate
Population: 3.5 million

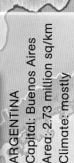

WESTERN EUROPE

Western Europe generally refers to the countries in the westermost half of Europe, although exact definitions vary.

SPAIN
Capital: Madrid
Area: 499,542 sq/km
Climate: temperate
Population: 41 million

Lisbon

Madrid

Bullfighting is still passionately followed in Spain.

Spain

Spain dominates most of the Iberian Peninsula in southwest Europe. The landscape is dominated by high plateaus with mountain ranges. The nation was a dominant force in Europe during the 16th and 17th centuries. Bull fighting remains a major attraction, despite increasing opposition to its cruelty.

FRANCE
Capital: Paris
Area: 545,630 sq/km
Climate: cool winters and mild summers
Population: 64 million

The Eiffel Tower, Paris, is the tallest building in France and one of the world's most famous structures.

Paris

It took eight years and more than 430 construction workers to build Tower Bridge, London.

London

UNITED KINGDOM
Capital: London
Area: 241,590 sq/km
Climate: temperate
Population: 61 million

The United Kingdom

The North Sea and the English Channel separate the United Kingdom from the rest of Europe. The countries of England, Scotland, Wales, and Northern Ireland make up the United Kingdom. England is the region's most populous area with 49 million inhabitants.

GERMANY
Capital: Berlin
Area: 349,223 sq/km
Climate: temperate
Population: 82 million

Amsterdam

Rome

Ljubljana

Vienna

Prague

Berlin

Alpine countries

Alpine states refer to the countries associated with the Alps region. As defined by the Alpine Convention of 1991, the region of the Alps comprises of the territories of seven countries. These seven states of the Alps are Switzerland, Liechtenstein, Austria, Slovenia, Germany, France and Italy.

Fun Facts

Belgium is nicknamed 'the battlefield of Europe' and 'the cockpit of Europe' due to its strategic role in the World Wars.

NORTHERN EUROPE

Northern Europe is a loose term that generally includes the Nordic countries of northernmost Europe, including: Sweden, Finland, Iceland, Denmark and Norway.

Sweden

Sweden is a highly successful and peaceful northern European country with high levels of literacy and employment. It is the third biggest country in the European Union by landmass, with about 85 percent of the people residing in urban areas. The landscape is mostly low and flat.

Norway

Norway is partitioned by mountains and has a fjord-rich shoreline that is over 21,000 km (13,050 miles) long. Its merchant and oil fleets are among the world's largest. This country of over 4.6 million boasts an extremely high literacy rate.

Finland

Finland, in northern Europe, has a mountainous landscape in the north and is low-lying in the centre and the south. The population is mostly concentrated in the triangle formed by the cities of Tampere, Turku, and Helsinki. The country is home to over 180,000 lakes well complemented by rich coniferous forests.

FINLAND
Capital: Helsinki
Area: 304,473 sq/km
Climate: cold to temperate
Population: 5.2 million

The whooper swan is the national bird of Finland.

Helsinki

Stockholm

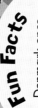
This Sami Teepee is the Norwegian version of the Native American tent.

SWEDEN
Capital: Stockholm
Area: 410,934 sq/km
Climate: diverse (temperate to cold)
Population: 9 million

Oslo

NORWAY
Capital: Oslo
Area: 307,442 sq/km
Climate: temperate to cool
Population: 4.6 million

Fun Facts

Denmark once controlled the whole of northern Europe and was a very important power. It is where the play *Hamlet* by William Shakespeare is set.

DID YOU KNOW?

Sweden is connected to Denmark in the south by the Öresund Bridge, the longest combined road and rail bridge in Europe.

101

CENTRAL EUROPE

Central Europe is the region lying between the defined areas of Eastern and Western Europe. It includes the countries of Estonia, Latvia, Lithuania, Poland, Slovakia, Czech Republic and Hungary.

Czech Republic

The Czech Republic consists of the regions of Moravia and Bohemia. Moravia is mostly hills and lowlands and lies to the east; Bohemia is more of a plateau and is surrounded by mountains. The castles and palaces in the country are a wonderful attraction to tourists.

The Tatra mountains form a natural border between Poland and Slovakia

Prague

CZECH REPUBLIC
Capital: Prague
Area: 77,276 sq/km
Climate: temperate
Population: 10.2 million

HUNGARY
Capital: Budapest
Area: 92,340 sq/km
Climate: temperate
Population: 10 million

Budapest

Warsaw

POLAND
Capital: Warsaw
Area: 304,459 sq/km
Climate: temperate to cold
Population: 38.5 million

Estonia

A republic in northeastern Europe on the Baltic Sea, Estonia is the smallest of the Baltic States. Curiously, it has the highest ratio of meteorite craters to land area in the world and it is also one of the most sparsely populated countries in Europe.

Hungary

The Danube River flows north to south and cuts landlocked Hungary almost in half. The Hungarians migrated from Asia more than a thousand years ago. The culture is, thus, distinct from countries around it that are dominated by Germanic and Slavic peoples.

Vilniusa

Riga

Tallinn

Riga in Latvia is well-known for its beautiful, distinctive architecture.

ESTONIA
Capital: Tallinn
Area: 43,211 sq/km
Climate: moderate winters, temperate summers
Population: 1.3 million

Fun Facts

The traditional houses in Slovakia, which are mostly wooden houses, are painted with designs based on traditional embroidery from the region.

SOUTHEASTERN EUROPE

The Balkan region in southeastern Europe takes its name from the Balkan Mountains, which run from Bulgaria into eastern Serbia.

Romania

On the Black Sea coast of southeastern Europe lies the country of Romania. The country is divided into three major regions—Wallachia in the south, Moldavia in the northeast, and Transylvania at the centre. Though the majority of the population is Romanian, there is a fair population of Hungarians too.

Greece

People have lived in Greece for more than 5,000 years. Its civilisation started about 2,500 years ago. The country of Greece has many islands. Some of its earlier people wrote plays that are still performed today. Greece is also known for its sculptures.

Fun Facts

The ancient ritual of barefooted dancing on smouldering embers, emerged in several remote villages in the Strandzha Mountains, in Bulgaria.

Slovenia

Slovenia is a state in central Europe and was once a part of Yugoslavia. Slovenia won its independence in June 1991, after a ten-day battle with the Yugoslav army. Of all the independent nations of the former Yugoslavia, Slovenia is the most prosperous, with the highest living standards.

ROMANIA
Capital: Bucharest
Area: 230,340 sq/km
Climate: temperate
Population: 22.2 million

CROATIA
Capital: Zagreb
Area: 56,414 sq/km
Climate: **Mediterranean** and **continental**
Population: 4.5 million

BULGARIA
Capital: Sofia
Area: 110,550 sq/km
Climate: temperate
Population: 7.2 million

GREECE
Capital: Athens
Area: 130,800 sq/km
Climate: temperate
Population: 10.7 million

The Bran castle is a national monument of Romania.

The Parthenon in Athens, Greece.

Bucharest

Sofia

Belgrade

Sarajevo

Tirane

Zagreb

Athens

NORTH AFRICA

Africa is the world's second-largest and second most-populated continent after Asia. North Africa is the northernmost region of the African continent, separated from the rest of Africa by the Sahara Desert.

Egypt

Egypt is one of the most populated countries in Africa and the Middle East. A great majority of the people live near the banks of the River Nile. Egypt is famous for its ancient civilisation and some of the world's most famous monuments, including the pyramid of Giza and its Great Sphinx. The terrain is dominated by deserts. The east is home to mountainous deserts, and the west has a drier desert. The Sahara lies to the south.

Rabat

Tripoli

LIBYA
Capital: Tripoli
Area: 1.75 million sq/km
Climate: Mediterranean to dry
Population: 6.3 million

Dakar

Abuja

Camel trekking in North Africa.

Fun Facts

Although it is situated in North Africa, Morocco is the only African country that is presently not a member of the African Union.

EGYPT
Capital: Cairo
Area: 995,450 sq/km
Climate: desert
Population: 83 million

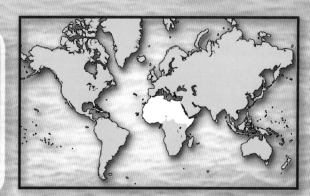

The famous
Sphinx and
pyramids, Egypt.

○ Cairo

○ Khartoum

Sudan

Much of Sudan is a hot, dry place where nomads herd camels and sheep. Sudan's traditional dress, the jalabia, is a loose fitting robe well suited to desert conditions. It is usually worn with a large scarf and a thobe, which is a type of long shirt.

SUDAN
Capital: Khartoum
Area: 2.38 million sq/km
Climate: tropical to desert
Population: 41 million

● Addis Ababa

Libya

Libya is blessed with oil, but it lacks water. It is the country with the highest per capita income in the continent. The population is mainly concentrated in its two major cities, Tripoli and Banghazi. Libya's Great Man-Made River Project is the biggest of its kind in the world, helping the **coastal** cities get much-needed water.

ETHIOPIA
Capital: Addis Ababa
Area: 1.12 million sq/km
Climate: tropical monsoon
Population: 85 million

DID YOU KNOW?

Ethiopia is Africa's largest coffee producing country and the second largest producer of cut flowers in Africa.

CENTRAL AND SOUTHERN AFRICA

Central Africa is the heart of the African continent. It includes Burundi, the Central African Republic, Chad, Republic of the Congo, and Rwanda. Southern Africa consists of the Republic of South Africa, Zimbabwe and Namibia.

Burundi

This small nation is located southeast of the equator. Though small in size, it has a dense population. Agriculture is the dominant occupation, with 90 per cent of the population being farmers.

South Africa

The Republic of South Africa is a country located at the southern tip of the continent of Africa. South Africa is known for its great diversity in cultures, languages, religious beliefs and ethnic groups. For many years South Africa had a system of Apartheid, where racial groups were separated, but this was abolished in 1994, to great celebration worldwide.

REPUBLIC OF THE CONGO
Capital: Brazzaville
Area: 341,500 sq/km
Climate: tropical
Population: 4 million

Fun Facts

The country of Rwanda has a hill-dominated landscape. Because of this, it is nicknamed the 'land of a thousand hills'.

DID YOU KNOW?

The presence of important minerals like cobalt, copper, diamonds, gold, silver, tin and coltan makes the Congo one of Africa's most mineral-rich countries.

CHAD
Capital: Ndjamena
Area: 1.25 million sq/km
Climate: tropical and desert
Population: 10.3 million

Ndjamena

The Congo is rich in its wildlife.

Brazzaville

The African lion is mostly found in southeast Africa.

Luanda

Chad

Chad is a landlocked nation with a diverse landscape. An arid centre and a desert-dominated north sit alongside the fertile south.
Chad has had an unstable few decades — primarily due to tension between the Arab-Muslim north and east and the African-Christian south.

ANGOLA
Capital: Luanda
Area: 124 million sq/km
Climate: diverse (semi-arid to hot)
Population: 12.8 million

Harare

The semi-nomadic Masaai can be found in Tanzania and Kenya.

Pretoria

Maputo

SOUTH AFRICA
Capital: Pretoria
Area: 1.21 million sq/km
Climate: mostly semi-arid
Population: 49 million

MIDDLE EAST

The Middle East spans the whole of southwestern Asia and northeastern Africa. It has a dry and hot climate. Countries in the Middle East include Iraq, Iran, Israel, UAE, Kuwait and Jordan.

Jeruselam

Amman

The Western, or Wailing Wall is one of the most sacred places for people of Jewish faith.

ISRAEL
Capital: Jeruslam
Area: 20,330 sq/km
Climate: temperate
Population: 7.2 million

JORDAN
Capital: Amman
Area: 91,971 sq/km
Climate: mostly arid
Population: 6.3 million

Iran

Iran is a country full of mountains and deserts. Desert areas dominate the east of the country. Farming is primarily concentrated in the narrow plains or valleys in the north and west – places more likely to get rainfall. The oil reserves lie in the southwest.

Mecca is considered the centre of the Islamic faith.

Israel

The eastern interior of Israel is dry and includes the lowest point on the Earth's surface – the Dead Sea. The majority of the population is Jewish, with a minority Arab population.

Fun Facts

Iran is one of the world's oldest continuous major civilisations, with historical and urban settlements dating back to 4,000 BC.

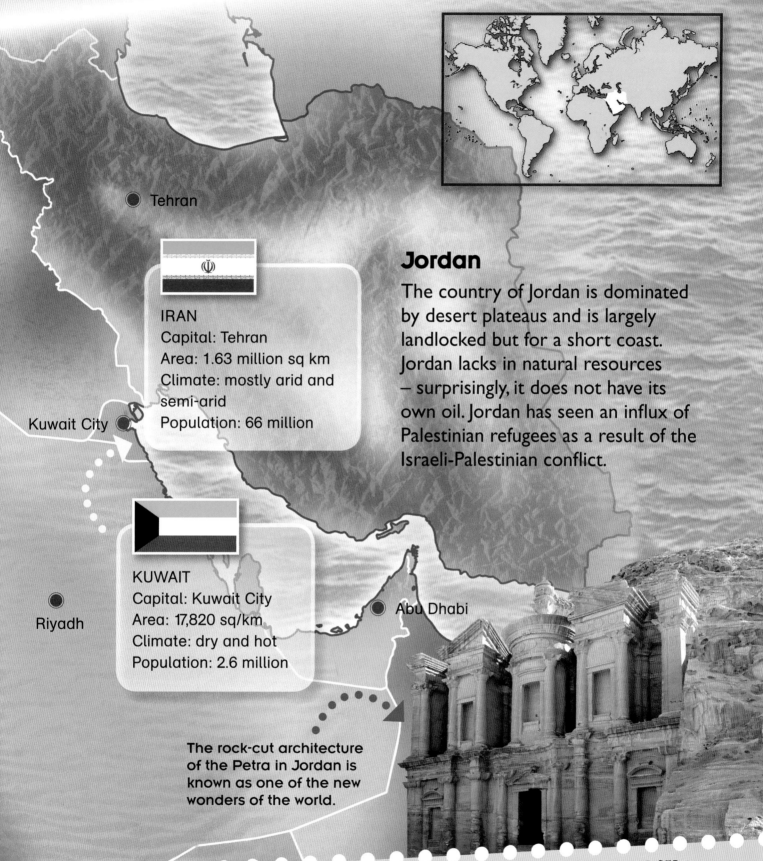

Tehran

IRAN
Capital: Tehran
Area: 1.63 million sq km
Climate: mostly arid and semi-arid
Population: 66 million

Kuwait City

KUWAIT
Capital: Kuwait City
Area: 17,820 sq/km
Climate: dry and hot
Population: 2.6 million

Riyadh

Abu Dhabi

The rock-cut architecture of the Petra in Jordan is known as one of the new wonders of the world.

Jordan
The country of Jordan is dominated by desert plateaus and is largely landlocked but for a short coast. Jordan lacks in natural resources – surprisingly, it does not have its own oil. Jordan has seen an influx of Palestinian refugees as a result of the Israeli-Palestinian conflict.

DID YOU KNOW?

Kuwait was the first Arab country in the Gulf to have an elected parliament.

109

RUSSIA AND NEIGHBOURING COUNTRIES

Russia is the largest country in the world in terms of area. Its neighbours include Kazakhstan, Turkmenistan, Ukraine, Moldova, and Uzbekistan, among others.

The St. Basil's Cathedral is about 450 years old.

Moscow

RUSSIA
Capital: Moscow
Area: 16.99 million sq/km
Climate: Diverse (warm to extremely cold)
Population: 140 million

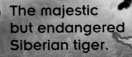

The majestic but endangered Siberian tiger.

Russia

Founded in the 12th century, Russia established worldwide power and influence to become the largest socialist state and a recognised superpower. Russia has many attractions, from freshwater lakes, soaring mountains, rivers and forests to beautiful and rich wildlife.

KAZAKHSTAN
Capital: Astana
Area: 2.66 million sq/km
Climate: continental
Population: 15.3 million

Kazakh people can be found in China and Mongolia as well.

Astana

UZBEKISTAN
Capital: Tashkent
Area: 425,400 sq/km
Climate: hot summers, mild winters
Population: 27.5 million

Bishkek

Tashkent

Kazakhstan

Kazakhstan is a country in central Asia and Eastern Europe. It is ranked as the ninth largest country in the world as well as the world's largest landlocked country. Kazakhstan is famous for the Baykonur Cosmodrome or space station.

Uzbekistan

Uzbekistan is central Asia's most populated nation. About 80 per cent of the country is dominated by the Qizilqum desert, with mountain ranges present in the southeast and the northeast of the country. The Fergana Valley lies to the country's northeast and is its most developed and fertile region, containing many industries.

The brown bear is one of the top predators in the jungles of Russia.

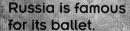

Russia is famous for its ballet.

Fun Facts

The Voronya Cave, situated in Georgia, is the deepest known cave in the world.

DID YOU KNOW?

Armenia is home to a leading centre of metallurgy, the scientific study of metal and its properties.

CHINA AND NEIGHBOURING COUNTRIES

China is the most populous country in the world and one of the biggest. Its neighbours include Japan, Singapore, Mongolia and Cambodia, among others.

Ulan Bator ●

The home to the nomadic Mongol.

China

China is the third largest country in the world. It is also one of the world's oldest civilisations with a history of more than 7,000 years. The landscape is diverse, with hills, plains, mountains, and deltas. The climate ranges from hot tropical in the south to subarctic in the northeast.

CHINA
Capital: Beijing
Area: 9.32 million sq/km
Climate: diverse
(tropical to very cold)
Population: 1.3 billion

Paddy fields — a feature of rice-growing China.

Fun Facts

Mongolia is the seventh largest country in Asia in terms of area. The country is totally landlocked, with China on one side and Russia on the other.

112

South Korea

South Korea comprises the southern half of the Korean peninsula, and numerous islands off the southern and western coasts. The landscape is full of mountains, though less in number than in North Korea.

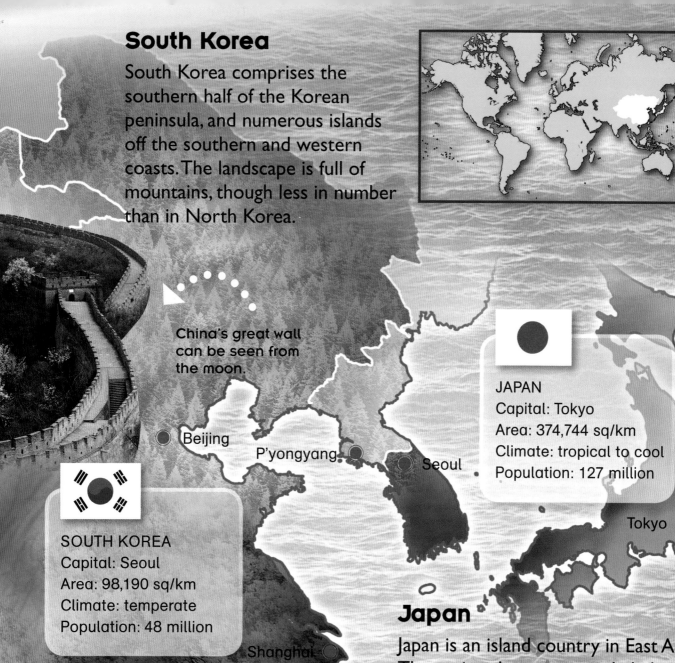

China's great wall can be seen from the moon.

Beijing

P'yongyang

Seoul

SOUTH KOREA
Capital: Seoul
Area: 98,190 sq/km
Climate: temperate
Population: 48 million

JAPAN
Capital: Tokyo
Area: 374,744 sq/km
Climate: tropical to cool
Population: 127 million

Tokyo

Shanghai

Taipei

Japan

Japan is an island country in East Asia. The ancient Japanese people believed theirs was the first land awakened by the rising sun. The Japanese call their land Nippon, meaning 'land of the rising sun'. It is believed that only 18 percent of Japan's land is suitable for **settlement**, which explains the over-populated cites!

DID YOU KNOW?

In the Gobi Desert of Mongolia fossilised dinosaur remains were found in 1920s, as well as the first dinosaur egg.

THE INDIAN SUBCONTINENT

The subcontinent comprises India, Pakistan, Nepal, Bhutan, Bangladesh and Sri Lanka.

Kabul

Islamabad

Beautiful mosques like this one are abundant in Pakistan.

New Delhi

The Taj Mahal is one of India's most beautiful monuments.

PAKISTAN
Capital: Islamabad
Area: 778,720 sq/km
Climate: mostly hot
Population: 176 million

Mumbai

India

India is the biggest country in the subcontinent and has the second largest population in the world. India's physical, religious and racial variety is reflected in its culture. This vast cultural diversity is reflected in its religious **monuments** — temples, mosques, churches, monasteries, gurudwaras etc.

INDIA
Capital: New Delhi
Area: 2.97 million sq/km
Climate: tropical monsoon to temperate
Population: 1.1 billion

Chennai

Colombo

Pakistan

The eastern and southern parts of the country have the Indus River and its tributaries; most of the population is concentrated along these areas. West of the river, the land is dry and mountainous. To the north lies K2, the tallest mountain in the world after Everest.

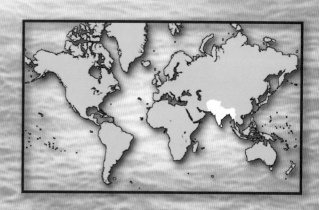

Sri Lanka

Sri Lanka is a tropical island nation that lies at the southernmost tip of India. Most of the well-renowned tea plantations are found at the centre of the country. The Sinhalese community constitutes the majority of the population, while the Tamils dominate the minority. The southwest is the most densely populated, and it is here that you can find Colombo, the country's capital.

Fun Facts

Many of the houses in Bangladesh are often raised on stilts or embankments to help protect them from flooding.

Dhaka

Kolkata

BANGLADESH
Capital: Dhaka
Area: 133,910 sq/km
Climate: tropical
Population: 156 million

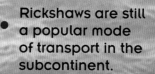

Rickshaws are still a popular mode of transport in the subcontinent.

DID YOU KNOW?

Eight of the highest peaks of the world, including Mount Everest, are situated in Nepal.

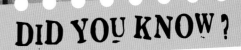

SOUTHEAST ASIA

Southeast Asia lies south of China, east of India and north of Australia. The region is known for earthquakes and tremors (seismic activity) because several geological plates meet here.

Hanoi

VIETNAM
Capital: Hanoi
Area: 325,360 sq/km
Climate: diverse
(tropical to dry)
Population: 87 million

THAILAND
Capital: Bangkok
Area: 511,770 sq/km
Climate: tropical
Population: 66 million

Thailand

The Chao Phraya River basin dominates the country of Thailand. Bangkok, the country's capital, lies in this basin. East Thailand is mainly woodlands and grasses. The southern region is full of hills and is well forested. Northern Thailand has the highest mountains.

Bangkok

Phnom Penh

The Petronas Towers are two of the tallest buildings in the world.

MALAYSIA
Capital: Kuala Lumpur
Area: 328,550 sq/km
Climate: tropical
Population: 26 million

Kuala Lumpur

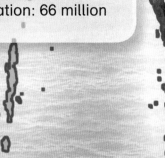

Vietnam

Vietnam is 1,600 km (1,000 miles) long from north to south and is extremely narrow – just 40 km (25 miles) wide at its narrowest. The Red River and the Mekong River dominate the landscape. Hanoi is the main city of the Red River, and Ho Chi Minh is the main city of the Mekong River.

Cambodia

Cambodia is mostly covered with forests. Once a war zone in the latter half of the 20th century, the country enjoys greater stability these days. **Subsistence farming** is still the predominant means of earning.

Manila

An exotic Bali dancer.

Fun Facts

The Petronas Towers in Malaysia are the world's tallest twin buildings and were the tallest buildings in the world until Taipei 101 was built.

DID YOU KNOW ?

Indonesia is a transcontinental country spanning Southeast Asia and Oceania, comprised of more than 17,000 islands!

AUSTRALIA AND NEIGHBOURING COUNTRIES

Australia is a country in the southern hemisphere. Australasian countries include New Zealand, East Timor, Solomon Islands and Papua New Guinea.

Settlement in Australia

Aboriginal settlers arrived on the continent from Southeast Asia about 40,000 years before the first Europeans began exploration in the 17th century. Six colonies were created in the late 18th and 19th centuries. Today, Australia is one of the most popular destinations for tourists.

Papua New Guinea

Papua New Guinea, in the Southwest Pacific, is one of the most diverse countries in the world. This largely unexplored nation has over 850 indigenous languages.

AUSTRALIA
Capital: Canberra
Area: 7.6 million sq/km
Climate: arid to semi-arid
Population: 21 million

The red kangaroo is the national animal of Australia.

Perth

DID YOU KNOW

The world's largest saltwater lagoon, Marovo Lagoon, is situated in New Georgia, Solomon Islands.

PAPUA NEW GUINEA
Capital: Port Morseby
Area: 452,860 sq/km
Climate: tropical
Population: 6 million

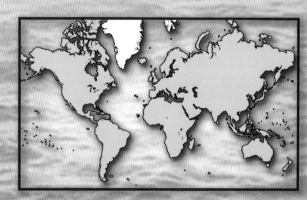

SOLOMON ISLANDS
Capital: Honiara
Area: 27,540 sq/km
Climate: tropical
monsoon
Population: 600,000

Rugby, the country's national game, is followed passionately in New Zealand.

The Sydney Opera House stages up to 2,500 art performances and events each year.

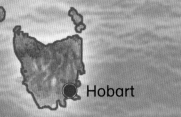

Sydney

Canberra

Melbourne

Hobart

New Zealand

New Zealand is an island country in the south-western Pacific Ocean. It has two main landmasses, the North Island and the South Island, and numerous smaller islands. The original Maori inhabitants named New Zealand Aotearoa, meaning 'the land of the long white cloud'. The indigenous, flightless kiwi is the country's national bird.

NEW ZEALAND
Capital: Wellington
Area: 268,021 sq/km
Climate: temperate
Population: 4.2 million

Wellington

119

THE POLES AND GREENLAND

The Earth, like a magnet, has two poles – the North Pole and the South Pole. These regions are dominated by the polar ice-caps, resting on the Arctic Ocean and the continent of Antarctica.

North Pole

The Earth's North Pole is covered by a floating pack of ice over the Arctic Ocean. The land from the North Pole down to the northern forests is known as the Tundra. Despite the extreme climate, animals that survive and make the Tundra their home include polar bears, Arctic hares and Arctic foxes.

The fur of the Arctic fox turns grey-brown during summer.

The polar bear is an accomplished swimmer and is often found at sea.

GREENLAND
Capital: Nuuk
Area: 2.16 million sq/km
Climate: extreme cold
Population: 57,600

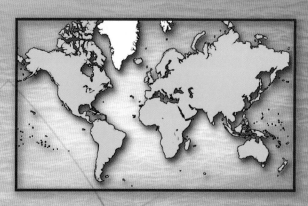

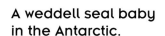

The penguin is one of the few living creatures thriving in the Antarctic.

A weddell seal baby in the Antarctic.

South Pole

The landmass of the Earth's South Pole (or Antarctica) is covered by the Antarctic ice sheet. Seventy per cent of the fresh water on Earth can be found in this ice sheet. The South Pole is much colder than the North Pole as it receives less solar radiation.

Greenland

Greenland is one of the world's largest island, but it is not classified as a continent. Geographically a part of North America, its history is dominated by Denmark, Norway and Iceland.

Fun Facts

There are no permanent human residents in Antarctica because of the freezing cold.

DID YOU KNOW

Less rain falls annually in Antarctica than in the Sahara Desert!

GLOSSARY

Adapt: to change according to the situation and circumstance

Endangered: something that is in danger of vanishing from the Earth

Gills: respiratory organ of animals that live in water

Hump: something that bulges out

Migrate: move from one region to another

Nocturnal: animals that are active during the night

Offspring: babies; the young of an animal

Predator: animal that hunts

Primate: an animal group that includes monkeys

Self defence: to protect oneself

Serrated: having a row of sharp, saw-like teeth

Venom: poisonous substance

secreted by some animals

Vibration: move back and forth in a rapid manner

Asteroids: floating rocks in space that move around the Sun

Axis: imaginary line around which the Earth rotates

Camouflage: disguise

Dense: something thick where very little light can pass through

Equator: imaginary line around the centre of the Earth

Evolution: process by which something changes over time

Excretion: process of discharging unnecessary waste matter from the body

Earthquake: shaking and vibration of the Earth's surface

Gravity: force of attraction

GLOSSARY

between two bodies

Hemisphere: Half of the Earth – divided into Southern and Northern Hemispheres

Photosynthesis: process by which plants use sunlight to make their food

Reproduction: process of producing young, by birth or other method

Shoreline: boundary between water and land

Biodiversity: range of plants and animals living in a specific area

Coastal: relating to or of a coast

Continental: something typical of mainland Europe

Diverse: different and many

Earth: planet where we live

Himalayas: a 2,400 km (1,500 mile) mountain range in India and Tibet

Indigenous: originating where it was found

Landlocked: surrounded by land

Landscape: all the visible features of an area

Mediterranean: related to or near the Mediterranean Sea

Monuments: historical structures

Natural Resource: resources found in nature

Rockies: mountain range of western North America

Settlement: area where a group of people live together

Subsistence farming: farming that produces food enough for a farmer's family

INDEX

INDEX